Your Magnetic Energy

Finding the Power to Become More

Dan Hoeger

Central Park South Publishing
New York, New York

ISBN: 978-1-0878-6337-5

Cover Design: Judy Corcoran

Printed in the United States, March 2020

DEDICATION

I dedicate this book to the people who represent the essence of the success and happiness I have experienced in life. Namely, Rosie, my wife and my soul mate for the past 50 years, my six adult children, their wonderful spouses, and the 13 beautiful grandchildren they have blessed Rosie and me with. Thank you all for your love and support during every stage of my life and career.

I would be remiss if I did not also give a special thanks to Linda Langton of Langton's International Literary Agency and Central Park South Publishing. The prompting and challenging she and her staff provided to me during the writing and editing of this book played a major role with it becoming a reality.

Table of Contents

Introduction

Regardless of who we are or where we are at in our journey, the fact is, we are all in search of that something that we can best describe as becoming "more." Maybe that more relates to our financial security. Or perhaps it's success in our careers or business. Maybe the "more" we are in search of involves a deeper relationship with that certain someone, or perhaps it entails our spirituality. Regardless of how you may define your becoming "more," it is the obtaining this "more," by generating our Magnetic Energy, is what the message of this book is all about.

In an easily readable and down to earth conversational style, this book leads readers to the realization that everyone already has the talents and abilities to pursue their chosen life. To achieve the life we want and the destination we aspire, we must first recognize and then take control of the talents that have been entrusted to us. In other words, we need to polish and shine those rough diamonds we already possess.

Throughout these pages, ideas and suggestions are offered on how we can best identify, develop, and then build upon our talents so to become the best rendition of ourselves that will permit us to achieve the success, satisfaction, and fulfillment we seek in all aspects of our life.

The theme and focused message of this book is to provide various avenues for the journey toward becoming our best rendition. Toward that goal this book builds upon and continually promotes the reality that it is through our Positive Thinking that we establish the foundational blocks of Faith, Trust, and Confidence so to provide the emotional convictions necessary to generate the inspiration we need for our journey to achieve what we are indeed capable of. Without that foundation, Positive Thinking, by itself, is reduced to only wishful thinking. As we are all aware, wishing alone will not accomplish anything. This book promotes the fact that if we are determined to reach the destination of our journey that Positive Thinking is only a part of the equation.

For most of us, although our careers are an essential aspect of our life, our success, fulfillment, and self-satisfaction will often be determined by the path we take with our lives in general. Because real and sustainable success encompass our entire identity, this book will further focus on many of the traits that make us who we are, both professionally and personally.

Readers will come to an understanding of why success is much more than a career position, a lofty title, or driving a fancy car. True success has much more to do with becoming the best rendition of ourselves as we were meant to be. Success is when we can say, "*I have become the person I had always wanted to be, and I have accomplished what I aspired to.*" Achieving this level of success is when we become our true self and the best rendition of ourselves as we were created to be.

Success in all aspects of our life is a journey, a journey that hopefully makes us better today than we were yesterday. It's a journey of which our destiny will be determined by the focus and priorities we have for our life.

Because of the personal nature of our upbringing, our value system, and our priorities, success cannot be viewed as a "one size fits all." We can thank God for that. The world would be a sad and boring place to live if that were the case. Therefore, at the onset, a definition of success is proposed that will have meaning to everyone from the corporate executive to the minister, and from the politician to the schoolteacher. In other words, how each of us experiences success is predicated more by the journey we chose than it is by the mere attainment of fame, fortune, position, or power.

This book provides thoughts and concepts of numerous time-tested methods intended to motivate our psyche and regenerate our energy to maintain maximum power for us to become and do our best. But more than merely providing the "how to," this book stresses the importance of the "why."

Because that "why" is such an important factor in our motivation, we will discuss the mindset of those who have attained a level of sustainable success. In this way we can arrive to a better understand of the "why" they do what they do, and it is this "why" that resulted in the success they reached. Although the "how to" is always important, it is the "why" that supplies the motivation and determination to become our best. It is the "why" that ignites the spark that will lead to become all we were meant to be.

The fact that you have picked up this book and are investing your time reading the introduction is evident that you either have a desire to improve and advance your state in life or are searching for ideas to help someone you care about. Regardless if it's your life, someone in your family, a friend, employees, or a business associate, you will find the thoughts and suggestions inspirational, down to earth, practical and attainable.

So, now the question remains "what about the messenger?" Does the messenger have the credentials to deliver such a meaningful and powerful life-changing message?

I am a firm believer that the best messenger is one who has lived the message, and I think you will agree that I have done just that.

I began my business career at the tender age of 18 as a Kirby Vacuum Cleaner Salesman. By the time I was 22 years old I was the owner of the regional Factory Franchise and had opened offices in four different cities.

In 1972 I sold the business and entered the Real Estate Profession. For the next 35 plus years, my career had a primary focus in this arena as I progressed from that of a Salesperson to a Broker-Owner. In the early 80s my career evolved to that of a Real Estate Design/Build, General Contractor/Developer. At the time of my retirement, I was the President/CEO of a company that had built and developed projects throughout Eastern Iowa with sales that exceeding $80,000,000.

But let's stop there for a minute. In that short 145-word bio one could get the impression that my path of success was on a straight upward trajectory at about 45 degrees from zero to 100. But by no means was such the case.

The journey that took me from demonstrating a Kirby vacuum cleaner in a prospect's living room to the time of my retirement as president of a multi-million-dollar company incudes many details that this short bio fails to mention.

Details like the sometimes roller coaster of the highs and lows of business due to swings in both the national and local economy. Like for example the impact of the first oil shortage and gas crises, and the ensuing run-a-way inflation of the '70s. Or the swings that were caused by the banking crises of the '80s, followed by what is now termed as "The Great Recession."

Details like my missing, or maybe better yet, my refusing to accept the signs of changing trends in market conditions and consumer demands. Without a doubt, my 40-plus-year business journey was not without its challenges, and for sure not without my share of heartaches and heartbreaks. By no means did worry, anxiety, frustration, sleepless nights, and even several major financial and personal setbacks escape my journey.

A number years ago the television network ABC aired a top-rated program they entitled *The Wide World of Sports*. The famous tag line for this program was *"The thrill of victory and the agony of defeat."* I can assure you as the reader, during my 40-year business career I have experienced the thrill of victory more times than what I may have deserved. On the flip side, I had also made some horrendous mistakes along my journey, errors that at times cost me substantially, yet I do not think I have ever admitted to or resigned to defeat. Oh sure, at times I had my pity party and, on several occasions, even spent time grieving a loss. While at times I may have been down, I don't think I had ever considered myself as being out of the game.

So yes, I did pay my dues by spending time in the trenches, and yes, I have both the badges and scars to prove it. But that only validates part of my credentials.

It is estimated that during my 40-plus years in business I employed well over a thousand people in a variety of professional disciplines. Now as it relates to this book, this becomes important when one considers that to be successful it was necessary for me to keep both myself and my employees, of which I again remind you were from an array of professional disciplines, aptitudes, and personalities, all motivated to become and do our best.

As the employer, the boss, the leader, or the top dog in a small business (however you wish to describe the position), it can be somewhat different compared to that of the large corporate or institutional setting. Typically, in the corporate or institutional arena, one's advancement and success are more predicated on promotions of which come from those above. In the small business world, however, one's success is totally predicated on the success of those below.

Early in my business career, a wise mentor impressed upon me that my success would be dependent on the success of those on my staff. I was assured that the more I would help the individuals of my team to reach their goals, the more they would help me to achieve mine. It was this practice that I strived to perfect throughout my 40-year career. I believe it was this philosophy along with teaching and practicing the principles and guidelines as outlined in this book that enabled us to also enjoy a meager rate of employee turnover. It was this philosophy that helped me attain the success I had experienced.

But the message of this book does not resonate only with the small business owner. It's message also speaks loud and clear to the principal of the elementary and high school. The shop foreman in the local factory. The division leader in a software design firm. The sales manager or the salesperson of virtually any product or service. It can also provide invaluable advice and wisdom to anyone working hard to move ahead in their career, regardless of what their career aspirations may be. Becoming our best is a journey for us all, regardless of the position we may hold, the career path we may be on, or how we may describe that "best" to be.

The thoughts and suggestions I offer throughout this book are not merely theoretical, but instead are proven methods of success that I have not only studied and learned from some of the top experts in their field, but equally, and if not ever more critical, they are principles I have practiced and experienced myself.

I believe you will find that the book offers a timely, motivating, and meaningful message that will enable you also to enhance the journey to become all you can be.

1

Understanding Our Control

Maximizing the Value of This Book

Unlike fiction, this book is not intended to be one you can curl up with on a Sunday afternoon, read from cover to cover, and when completed, file on the shelf of your library and wait for the movie to come out.

The contents of this book are intended to speak to you directly about your career, your life, and your destiny. All of which, when packaged together, makes up who you are, and where you are heading. I am sure that you would agree that to say this is a very critical and essential subject is an understatement. Because the consequences of who you are and the direction you may be heading are vital to your destiny, it is strongly recommended that you become fully engaged with this book.

To do this, throughout you will be invited to make written notes of your thoughts, ideas, and facts about your career and life. In this way it will transfer the information from printed words on the pages of a book to that of being personal and tangible. This not only will allow you to follow the guidelines of the process as presented, but equally as important, it will be a way for you to record your thoughts and ideas that come to mind as to how this information can enhance both your career and life. If you are reading this book via Kindle or other electronic media, I would recommend that you have a notepad available for your written thoughts and ideas.

What Is Control?

Taking control of our talents and abilities is an essential aspect of becoming everything you want to become. But what does that control look like? For most of us, in all likelihood, we have one or two areas of our life that may require some fine-tuning. It's an area or areas that we would like to have more control of.

Let me share with you a little analogy about being in control.

Picture yourself sitting in the driver's seat of your car. You put the key in the ignition, and you start the engine as you have done thousands of times before. You feel ready to go. You feel as if you are in total control, in fact not only is this a feeling, it's an assumption that you give little or no thought to.

But then you start moving forward, and you suddenly discover that your front wheels are not responding to where you want them to go. You further realize that one front wheel wants to go in one direction, and the other in the opposite direction. Upon investigation, you find that one of your tie rods is broken. For those who may not know what a tie rod is; it's a small rod, which depending on the make and size of the vehicle, can be approximately one inch in diameter and about three to four feet in length. This tie rod connects the front wheels to the steering mechanism. Now this small broken rod, which consists of far less than say 1%, or maybe even 1/10th of 1% of the total makeup of the car, has removed all chance of any control you have in determining the direction your car will go.

The same could be said about life. Sometimes it can feel it's out of control. Although it may be only 1% that is out of whack, it's that 1% or less that can make us feel we have no control of anything.

If that 1% is a lack of control we have in our career, this will also adversely impact both our family life and our social life. As it often the case, as it transfers from our job to our personal and family life, that 1% tends to magnify itself, regardless of how much we try to keep it separate.

Chances are you have experienced the reality of having substantial stress due to a pressing deadline, or some especially challenging issue at work. The more crucial the deadline or difficulty of the problem, the higher our level of stress. But seldom do we leave that stress at the office. It becomes affixed in our mind to the point that it's all we can think about. Because it's weighing so heavy on our mind, we find it hard to have a meaningful conversation about anything else. We may even snap at anyone who demands our time or attention. At times we may also snap at them even if they are entitled to our attention. So yes, as it transfers from the office to our home, it often tends to magnify itself.

That same scenario applies if that 1% that is out of control is in our personal life. Again, we have all experienced how difficult it is to concentrate at work when we are facing a problematic issue at home. Whether it's an illness of a loved one, a relationship issue, or a personal financial crisis, we will usually discover that the more significant the impact the problem has on our lives, the more difficulty we will have in focusing on our job. So once again, as our crisis transfers from home to work, it often tends to magnify itself.

As a small business employer, it's common to develop a personal relationship with your employees. So, when employees are wrestling with personal problem of one sort or another, because of that personal relationship it's easy to see the impact it has on their professional productivity.

I can recall several occasions when a salesperson who would be going through a rough time in their marriage, and as a result found their sales production drop through the floor. More than once I heard such a salesperson state that their entire life was spinning out of control. In reality, it was not their "entire" life. It was a very important part yes, but their job was still the same. The needs of their clients had not disappeared. If they had children, their responsibility as a parent had not changed. I think you can get the point. Most of what was going on in their life had not changed. The one thing that had changed, however, was the degree of control, or I should say, lack of control they were experiencing in their marital relationship. Even though it was only one facet of their life, the more devastating that lack of control became, the more it would tend to carry over to other areas.

Of course, what can be even more devastating to all aspects of life is if we ignore that which is out of control and pretend that it does not exist.

Pretending that the tie rod on the car is not broken will not change anything. Even if I want to ignore or deny that it's broken, will not change the fact that the front wheels are pointing in different directions. The same can be said of our lives. Ignoring any area that may be out of tune will not change it.

When we are at home, trying to ignore a work problem only makes it fester on our mind all the more. When we are at work, trying to ignore a crisis we may be experiencing in our personal life seldom makes us more productive.

As I mentioned a bit earlier, while our ultimate intent in this book will be to enhance your professional career, to do this, we also need to include all aspects of life.

Let's begin with a little exercise. Take a minute and think about what is going on in your life right now. After reading each statement, I invite you to pause for a minute or so to reflect on where you are at in your life. Think about:

- Your career and the current position you hold
- Your personal finances
- Your relationships—both personally and professionally
- Your family and your social life
- Any other area of your life that comes to mind that is important to you

Now, of all these various areas of your life, I invite you to think of just one area, regardless of how major or minor it may be, that you feel you do not have as much control as you would like.

Before you have that knee-jerk reaction of saying that for you, life is totally under control, I would offer the following for you to consider.

✓ If you work for an employer, you may not have as much control as you think.

✓ If you have a staff or employees who work either for you or under your direction, the chances are that you may not have as much control as you think

✓ If your position requires you to deal directly with customers or clients, you may not have as much control as you think

✓ If you have children, especially if they are teenagers, you may not have as much control as you would like.

✓   If you have a spouse or a significant other in your life, I can almost guarantee you do not have any control, or for sure not as much as you may think you do. (Just kidding)

The above few examples don't even begin to include areas of our life such as our health, finances, job security, and so on.

I'm sure you get the point. Often, we like to think we have everything under control, but in this aspect, seldom will the reality of life correspond to what we would like to envision it to be.

Now let's again return to spend just a minute or so thinking about areas of your life in which you may not have as much control as you would like, as well as those areas where you feel it's essential to be in control. Record your thoughts in the space provided below, listing one or maybe two areas of your life that come to mind.

The one or two areas of my life that I would like to have, or need to have, more control over, could be best described as: _____

_____

_____

_____.

Now let's take that one step further. As you consider the one or two examples of areas in your life that you feel may be a bit out of control, or areas of your life that you would like to have more control of, I would now challenge you to consider what talents or abilities you may already possess that, if used effectively, could assist you in gaining or regaining control. If you don't feel that you already have what it takes to gain that control, I would then challenge you to consider which of your talents and abilities you already possess that could be further developed and strengthened that would permit you to regain control.

Why Control is Necessary

When I speak of the need to be in control, I'm not talking about becoming a so-called "control freak" with a need to control everyone and everything. That's not having control, that's merely a spoiled need to have things go your way. That type of control is usually counterproductive to bringing anything into balance.

What I am referring to is the control that we gain as a result of the responsibility that we accept for those areas of our life that will, to a great extent, determine the outcome of our career, our life, and our destiny.

To rephrase that, one could say: *The outcome of our career, our life, and our destiny will to a great extent be determined by the responsibility we accept for controlling that which is in our ability to control.* And that my friends most often will boil down to the degree of responsibility we accept for recognizing, developing, and using the talents and abilities with which we have been entrusted.

Regardless of what we do or who we are, we all have a desire to be successful at whatever objective we may undertake.

Of the thousands of people I have hired over the years, never once have I ever had anyone say to me, "Thanks for giving me this opportunity, but to be honest, I'm quite sure I won't be the success in this job to the degree that either of us would like."

Likewise, I have never heard of new parents, as they held their newborn infant in their arms, say, "Our goal is to be just average, run-of-the-mill parents."

When have you ever heard of a couple standing at the altar on the day of their wedding and each promising to be a second-rate spouse?

Just the opposite is true. In virtually every objective we undertake, our goal is to be as successful as we can.

Your Magnetic Energy

If I set out to mow the grass on a Saturday, my goal is to be a success at that objective.

If I play a round of golf, even though I know I am far from being a scratch golfer, still my goal is to be as successful as I can be.

Regardless of the goal, success will never be achieved unless we first accept the responsibility to take control of that which we can control, both in who we are, and what we become.

Now let's do another simple exercise.

- If your fairy godmother could wave her magic wand, and her fairy-tale pixie dust would fall upon you, and as a result, she could give you the power to have 100% control over your career, what then would your career look like?
- If she gave you 100% control over your life, what kind of life would you then have?
- If she gave you 100% control over your destiny, where would you see your life leading you?

I now invite you to enter your notes in the space provided below for each of these three areas consisting of your career, your life, and your destiny. Write a short sentence that would describe what each would look like if you had 100% control.

1. If I had 100% control over my career, my career would _____

_____

_____.

2. If I had 100% control over my life, it would be described as _____

_____

_____.

3. If I had 100% control over my destiny, what would that look like?

_____

_____

_____.

Now before we go any farther, we need to understand that what your fairy godmother gave you was control. She didn't help you to win the lottery. She didn't give you an increase in either the quality or quantity of your talents or abilities. She didn't make the entire world more submissive to your wants and needs. All she gave to you was control over those areas that are within your ability to control. You still have the responsibility to assume the control that she gave you. Before the career, the life, and the destiny that you had described above can become a reality; you must first accept the responsibility to put forth the energy and determination to use the talents and abilities you already possess so that you can assume the control she provided.

But now let's face reality. Absolute 100% control of any area of life may take that magic wand of a fairy godmother, for as we all know, in real life, having a total 100% control over anything is rare at best. However, regardless of the area, success never be achieved until we begin to focus on accepting the responsibility we have for controlling and using to the best of our abilities all the talent and skills at our disposal so that we can control as much of our life as possible.

As a rule, it's not so much that we don't have control; rather we simply have not taken control over those areas and situations of our life that are within our ability to control.

Adopting a Mindset

Therefore, if control is necessary to obtain the success that we desire, it's only logical then that it would be wise to study the type of control that people who have achieved a high degree of sustained success have taken in their lives. By exploring how they have taken responsibility for the control they have, and then by following in their footsteps, we also can significantly enhance our likelihood of being able to earn the success that we seek.

Consider the professional football coach and the amount of time that he, his staff, and his players spend each week repeatedly reviewing the tapes of the team they are about to face. The insight they receive from these tapes is not from focusing on what the other team did that was *wrong*; instead, the most value is always gained by studying and focusing on what the other side did that was *right*.

It is only when their primary focus is on the *success* of the other team that they will be able to prepare themselves to meet the challenges the other team will throw at them.

There is a story about Sam Walton, the founder of Walmart. The story goes that he would routinely walk the aisles of a competitor's store to see what they were up to regarding the "how" and the "what" they were selling, and how they were marketing it. It's said that one day Sam had one of his "lieutenants" with him. As they made their way through the store of their competitor, his associate was quick to point out all the areas he could criticize for what he felt were their downfalls. After a while, Sam stopped and told his lieutenant that his focus was on the wrong area. Sam said that he couldn't care less about what they were doing that was wrong, but he wanted to know what they were doing that was right.

Whether this story is true or not is not the point. The point is that if we want to improve our state of life, the best way to accomplish this is by focusing on the success of others and then attempting to apply their methods of success to our own life. By far the best way to imitate the achievements of others is not merely to learn *how* to do what they do, but rather, learn to *think* as they think. Only by first learning to *think* as they think can we begin to get a grasp on the *why*.

Consider the football team again. Seldom will the team study the tapes so they can discover a play that they have never seen or have not previously executed themselves? Rarely will the team, by watching the tapes, learn how to do something new. Instead, their desire is to get into the minds of the other side so the players can learn and understand the "why" the team executes the plays they do when they do.

Too often our mentality is, *"Teach me to do what that person is doing so I can be like them."* Although it is a given that "how" a person performs a task or objective is always important, however, if we truly wish to be "like" someone, then by far the best objective we can seek is to develop their same mindset.

Once we develop the mindset of those who are successful, then the execution of what they do will follow. But the opposite is not always the case. The simple act of "doing" by itself may not change our mindset. Oh, it may help over doing nothing at all, but by far the fastest and most direct route would be first to adopt their mindset.

Let me give you an example of the difference. When I was a young pup in the world of business, I had a mentor whom I truly admired. He had a very energetic and captivating personality. From my vantage point, he was successful in every area of his life. He had a life that I wanted to mimic. I wanted to be just like him. I wanted his success. Yes, I wanted a life like his.

From our many conversations, it was no secret that he was an early morning riser. He would often talk about getting out of bed by at least 5:00 AM. So naturally, if I wanted to be like him, I felt I also needed to do what he did, so I began to set my alarm for 5:00 AM.

Now, as I was born and raised on a farm with early morning chores, getting up that early was not foreign to me. But something was missing. Even though I was doing what he was doing, the critical point I was missing were the "whys" of why he was getting up at the time.

Maybe it was his morning ritual that I was missing. What if I also mimicked all he did between the time that his feet would hit the floor until he left for the office. If I did, that surly would fulfill what I felt I was missing. But the reality is that his entire morning ritual were mere actions that he performed. His rituals were merely something he did so even his routines did not explain the why. What it all boiled down to was that the *why* he got out of bed at 5 AM, and the *why* of his morning rituals was done to put his mind and body in the position that he could enthusiastically and energetically get a jump on his day. This enabled him to take full advantage of all that was at his disposal to be on his game every day.

The fact is, I could have continued to set my alarm and get up at 5 AM every day for the next 20 years and that may not have changed anything. I could have religiously performed every one of his morning rituals, but the fact also remains that until I could grasp the true *why* he got up that early, and the actual *why* he performed his morning rituals, the chances are that my life would not have changed to the degree I was seeking.

Therefore, instead of focusing on what successful people *do,* we will focus on developing the basic mindset that successful people have. That mindset that can best describe the *why.*

Definition of Success

Before we can have a meaningful discussion on the mindset of the successful person, it is critical for us to first arrive at a sound and reliable definition of what success means to us as individuals.

When I ask most any group in any of my seminars or retreats to give me their definition of a successful life, if there were 50 people in attendance, I would most likely get 50 different interpretations.

In most cases, we all define a successful life as being the life that we dream about—the "ideal" or the "epitome" of what we want our life to be.

Because we are individuals with different lives, lifestyles, and upbringings, with varying values and priorities, as well as diverse talents and abilities, one person's idea and definition of a successful life may not correlate with the next person's view.

And that is the way it is supposed to be. That's just part of what makes each of us a unique and special individual. We each have the priorities that we are dealing with in our life at this specific moment in our history. Depending on what those priorities may be, will determine what our definition of success may be.

For some of us, our highest priority at this juncture in our life will be that of our career. If that's the case, success for us will be defined as it relates to how we may advance or succeed in that area.

For the next person, his highest priority will be that of getting his personal finances under control. Therefore, success to him may be defined as having his bills paid or having a bit of a cushion with a little money in the bank.

For others, their highest priority will involve relationships, either those they have or would like to have. Success for them will be defined based on whatever that may entail.

Therefore, whenever we speak of success throughout this book, I want you to remember that I am talking directly to you and addressing your current individual priorities for the type of success that you are seeking.

Now it's time for another exercise. In the space provided below, I invite you to complete the following two sentences.

1. I will consider that I have reached my true definition of success in my career or professional life when I _____

_____

_____.

2. I will consider that I have reached my true definition of success in my personal life when I _____

_____.

After you have completed the above exercise, let's follow with another helpful exercise.

I now invite you to think of three different people and write their names in the spaces provided below. They can be individuals you know personally, by reputation, or even historical figures. If the individual you select is someone from history, I would suggest it be someone who has lived within the last 100 years or so.

First: Think of either a successful _political leader_ or a _military leader_ who you admire. Once you have that individual pictured in your mind, write that person's name here: _____

_____

Second: Think of a successful _religious or spiritual leader_ who you admire and again write the name here: _____

_____

Third: Think of a successful _sports figure_ who you admire and write that person's name here: _____

_____

As you think about these three people, chances are that each one achieved a level of success that surpassed most of their peers. However, chances are also equally as good that each of these three individuals would define success totally different, simply because each have different priorities, lives, hopes and dreams, personalities, and aptitudes.

Now let's take our thought process even one step further, I ask you to think of a successful *businessperson* who you admire and write the name here: _____

_____

I'm sure that this successful businessperson would also define success different from that of the previous three names on your list. Just like the other three, this businessperson also has individual priorities and reasons as to his or her focus on success.

While it is true that the details of success and the benefits of what success will reward us with is defined by each of us individually and are based on the priorities we have at a given point in our life, I still believe there is a definition that applies to each one of us as individuals. I think there is a definition that can also apply to us as individuals throughout our lives, regardless of our priorities. It is a definition that I feel quite comfortable stating that each of the four individuals whose names you wrote down earlier would agree with as well.

The definition of success that I am going to propose that we use throughout the book is as follows:

Success is a sustaining pattern of growth and improvement in one's life that leads to becoming our true self. A growth and improvement that is the result of us using to the very best of our capability all the talents and abilities we have been entrusted with to become our best rendition. A growth that will make us better today than we were yesterday. A growth that will produce a sense of fulfillment, satisfaction, and peace in who we are, what we are doing, and what we have become at this point in our life. © 2017 Dan Hoeger Seminars, LLC

Your Magnetic Energy

We often view success as only a future destination. We often say, "I want *to be* successful." We rarely say or even think to ourselves, "*I am successful.*" Seldom do we look at success as a present-day accomplishment. In fact, in some respects, it may even be viewed upon as being a bit boastful and egotistical by making such a statement, regardless if it is true or not. But read on.

While success can be a goal we strive for, it shouldn't be looked upon as only the final destination. Goals are to establish the target of where we want to go and how we are going to get there. Real success, on the other hand, should be viewed more like a journey. What a tragic life it would be for a person who waited until the end of their life before they found fulfillment, satisfaction, and peace in who they are and what they have become.

As we stated in our definition, "*success can be best described as being a journey that necessitates a pattern of growth. A growth and improvement that makes us better today than we were yesterday.*" Regardless of whether it encompasses our professional careers, our relationships, our spirituality, our finances, or who we are as a person, true success must be a journey of growth and improvement that we strive for continually. It's a growth and improvement that applies to each of us as individuals in all areas of our life, and during all stages of our life, and we must not compare our success to that of anyone else.

Now, let's review what you wrote earlier for your true definition of success in both your personal and professional life. I invite you to now identify which of the two has the highest priority to you currently. Select that one area that you have the greatest burning desire to succeed in. Be honest with yourself. Select what's in your heart. Not what you think it should be, or what you think others would say it should be.

It is that area that I would like for you to keep in focus as we discuss success throughout this book. As said earlier, whenever I speak of success, I invite you to picture that I am addressing you directly and referring to that specific area of success that you desire.

Whenever I refer to a successful person, I want you to imagine that I am referring to someone who has already attained the level of success that you desire in your life.

As we talk about the journey of success, I invite you to consider the journey you need to take to carry out that specific goal that you have identified as being your highest priority at this time.

But I also suggest that you keep in mind that attaining a specific success goal is not the destination, but only part of your journey.

As an example. In writing about your career success, let's say you said that you would have reached your definition of success when you have attained the position of Sr. VP of the company.

Imagine that today someone finally woke up and recognized your real talents and abilities, and as a result, by the end of this week you are promoted to that position. You would have finally made it. The job you worked so hard for is finally yours. If such was the case, would that mean because you had finally reached your goal and the success you wanted, you were now finished with life and could now take your ball and go home? No, that would not be the case at all! Receiving that promotion is only part of your journey. When we reach a long sought-after goal, it may put us on a new plateau in life, but in reality, we only begin a new journey!

But let's not just make that journey a hypothetical one. Let's bring it into real life. To do this, I invite you to list ten events or accomplishments in your past that you would identify as when you felt successful.

Regardless of whether it involved your personal life, such as when you met that certain someone, or the day you were married, or whatever. Or maybe the area of success you relate best to is in your professional career. No matter, I invite you to list ten successes you have experienced in your life. Again, have your list be all-encompassing and include success in all facets of your life.

I felt I was a successful or a success when I:

1. _____

2. _____

3. _____

4. _____

5. _____

6. _____

7. _____

8. _____

9. _____

10. _____

Take as much time as you need. Regardless of where you are in life, you should have no problem with listing at least 10 times that you would have described yourself as being successful. But don't limit your list to only 10. The more you can expand your list the better. Remember, these are your successes, regardless of how big or small. Don't evaluate your success by a comparison with anyone else. The fact is, there is not a person on this earth who cannot find someone who may be more successful, as well as many others who are not as successful.

Now as you review those successes that are a part of your life, also recall how each of them was an essential part of your journey. Once the victory was achieved, the chances are that you did not consider it your final destination. Each was merely a part of your continued journey of success. At the time and maybe even still today, that success was an essential part of the journey, and it's the journey that's important. It's the journey that will ultimately be defined and become the true definition of our success. It's the journey that will determine if we have become the best rendition of ourselves.

2

Understanding Our Purpose

Now let's continue our journey, and we do so with the understanding that we each have been created to fulfill a specific purpose and mission. To best accomplish our purpose and mission, we have been entrusted with our unique talents and abilities, and it is only when we both develop and use our talents and skills to their fullest that we can best fulfill our purpose and reason. Only by first discovering and then by fulfilling our purpose and mission can we hope to become the best rendition of ourselves.

With that understanding in hand, we will now focus on how to best accomplish our mission and the goal of utilizing our talents and abilities to their maximum potential.

Our talents and abilities are like the muscles in our bodies. If we don't use them, we will lose them. If we don't continue to develop them to become stronger, they will ultimately weaken and fade away completely.

For example, they say that once you learn to ride a bike you will never forget. While that may be true, I for one can assure you from personal experience that because I have not taken bike riding seriously for many years, I cannot ride a bike today like I did when I was 14!

A few years ago, one of our granddaughters, who was about five years old at the time, was visiting and was so proud that she was now taking gymnastics. She told me she had learned how to stand on her head. She proceeded to demonstrate her newly obtained skill, and, yes, she was quite good at it. After she had completed her task and I had complimented and praised her on how good she had done, I then told her that I also could stand on my head. After she chuckled at me, she then challenged me by saying, "OK, Papa, now you do it!"

Now I have stood on my head a thousand times, but I had not done it anytime recently. The truth be known, it had been quite some time. But what the heck. I know the mechanics of it and the "how" to do it, and that was all that was important . . . Right? Wrong! I not only broke the end table and tipped over a table lamp, but I also almost broke my neck in the process!

So, yes, I repeat—our talents and abilities are like our muscles in our bodies; if we don't use them, we will lose them. If we don't continue to develop them to become stronger, rust can and will soon set in, and they will ultimately weaken and fade away completely. The continued development of our talents and abilities is an essential aspect of our journey that must never be made light of.

Becoming More

If we desire to become more of either who we are or what we are doing, or even changing the direction we may be heading, we must first learn how to take control. Once we take control, we will soon discover that we can attain and obtain anything in life that we desire, provided of course that of which we want is in line with who we are, and that we become more effective in the efforts we put forth toward becoming the best rendition of ourselves.

It is a fact of life that we can only become the best version of ourselves when we focus on developing our talents and abilities to their very best. Our talents and abilities are personal and given to us specifically so we can accomplish our purpose in life. However, we receive them like that of a rough and unpolished diamond. It is our responsibility to transform and polish that rough diamond into the priceless jewel it is intended to be.

Always keep this firmly planted in your mind, the more we develop our talents and abilities the more of our true self we become. This leads to greater fulfillment and satisfaction that we will experience in what we do because of who we have become. That in turn, leads to a more profound passion that will produce the drive to become even more. This results in us doing yet even more, and the more we do, the more we will receive.

Earlier you listed four people from four different professions. These were individuals who had gained a level of respect and maybe even a degree of notoriety due to the success they attained in their life. To emphasize what I've just said in the last paragraph, let's rephrase that by using each point as it may apply to that of, say, the athlete you chose. For the sake of better visualization, I am going to use one of our local golf celebrities who has made it big on the national circuit. His name is Zach Johnson. I have no doubt many of you who follow golf have heard of him. Therefore:

1. *The more we develop our talents and abilities, the more of our true*

self we become.

Chances are when Zach first picked up the club and started playing the game, he viewed it as merely a sport he enjoyed. Then the more he played the game, the more he recognized that he was reasonably good at it. He began to acknowledge that he had a talent for the game that was a bit different, and maybe even a bit better from that of some of his friends.

Due to his enjoyment of the game and further recognizing his inborn talent, Zach began to put a greater emphasis on developing his skills and abilities by spending more time practicing at the driving range and the putting course. The more he practiced his game, the more he expanded his natural talents and abilities. This development continued to the point that he began to recognize just how good he was becoming, which evolved to the end of not only enjoying the game and being good at the game, but he also identified himself as *"being"* a golfer. And it was this "being" that also helped him realize this as an essential part of his true self and who he was as a person.

2. *Which leads to greater fulfillment and satisfaction that we will experience in what we do because of who we have become.*

The more Zach recognized his true self-identity as being a golfer, the more fulfillment and satisfaction he received in what he was doing.

3. *That, in turn, leads to a more profound passion that will produce the drive to become even more.*

The more Zach worked on developing his inborn talents and abilities for the game, the better golfer he became. This led to a greater enjoyment in what he was doing. This in turn developed into even a heightened passion he had for the game of golf, which then created an even greater desire to practice, with a determination to become even better at the game. This passion became the catalyst for him to focus on becoming the best rendition of himself, as the golfer he had grown to identify himself to be.

4. *This then results in us doing yet even more, and the more we do, the more we will receive.*

The more that Zach developed his inborn talents and abilities, the greater success he experienced. The more success he encountered, the higher his rewards became. All of which provided even a greater fulfillment and satisfaction with what he was doing, who he had become, and who he was now identifying himself to be. For Zach, he was on a journey to become the best rendition of himself.

To summarize: *the more we become and do, the more we will accomplish, and the more we accomplish, the more we will both have and become.*

Now I'm going to repeat that paragraph, this time, however, instead of looking at it from the perspective of Zach Johnson's career, I would invite you to view it from the perspective of the success priority you have for your life.

With this added insight, what does the statement mean for you in your specific situation when you read it to yourself? As you read each statement, I invite you to pause for a minute or so to reflect on each.

The more that I develop my talents and abilities, the more of my true self I will become.

This has led me to experience greater fulfillment and satisfaction in what I do because of my self-realization of who I am.

This has given me an even deeper passion that will produce the motivation for me to become even more.

The result of doing more is that the more I do, the higher the rewards that I will receive.

To carry this one step further, we need to reaffirm that, *"It is only when you first become more that you can expect to receive more."*

So, as it relates to the priority goal that you listed earlier, what do the words "become more" mean for you in your life?

Now I would ask that you relate that statement to *all* areas of your life.

What does it mean as it applies to your career? *"It is only when I first become more that I can expect to receive more."* In what ways do I need to become more if I wish to receive more from my career? Am I willing to put forth the effort toward becoming more to receive the "more" I am in search of?

What does it mean as it applies to your relationships? *"It is only when I first become more that I can expect to receive more."* How do I define the receiving more in my relationships? How would I describe becoming more and what do I need to further bring to my relationships to become more?

What does it mean as it applies to your spirituality? *"It is only when I first become more that I can expect to receive more."* How do I define spiritual growth for myself and how would I describe "becoming more" to achieve that growth I am searching for?

What does it mean when it comes to your finances, your social life, or whatever area of your life you may identify as important to you? *"It is only when I first become more that I can expect to receive more."* Regardless of the area of our life, if we wish to receive more, we must identify and then put forth the effort to become more.

We drill it into our memory even deeper by once again summarizing this by saying that *the more we become and do, the more we will accomplish, and the more we accomplish, the more we will both have and become.*

You see, it all works together in an ever-evolving, yet ever-so-widening spiral of success. But it all must begin with first having a focus and desire to become more. This is a critical step toward taking control of our career, our life, and our destiny.

The Wise Old Hermit

I am reminded of a fable I once heard regarding this very topic. It goes something like this.

Once upon a time, there was a young person *(man or woman . . . you decide who it should be as it could be either, but for this example, I'll say it's a young lad.)* who had a desire to achieve the highest level of success possible. He sought the advice of numerous elders in his community. Several times it was suggested that his best bet would be to seek the advice of a wise old hermit who lived high on the mountain. Finally, he decided to do just that. He packed his backpack, and off he set in search of the hermit.

For many days he searched and searched until finally he came upon a clearing, and there he found the hermit.

Now picture this in your mind. Here is this old man sitting by a small fire pit located outside the cave where he lived. He had an old olive drab colored wool blanket around his shoulders. His hair was over his shoulders and still had some straw in it from sleeping on his makeshift straw mattress. His beard was long and in an unkept state. And yet this is the guy our young man had been searching for to learn the secret of success.

But what the heck, he came this far. So, after introducing himself, the young lad told the hermit that he wanted to learn the secret to achieving great success.

The wise old hermit told him that before he could achieve the success he was seeking, he first needed to understand that there are two goddesses who reside deep within the heart of each one of us: One goddess is the Goddess of Wealth, and the other is *the* Goddess of Personal Improvement.

The wise old hermit assured the young lad that although both would love him dearly, the rule was such that he could only pursue one to the exclusion of the other. He gave the young man the instruction that whichever goddess he elected to pursue; it would be that goddess that he would need to give his total attention to.

But, said the wise old Hermit to the young man, "Here's the secret that you need to understand. If you pursue the Goddess of Wealth, she will be delighted and pleased with you, because she unquestionably loves to be chased and pursued. Just know that the more you pursue her, the more she will tease you and make you chase after her. The more you chase after her, the more she will attempt to elude you."

"However," said the old hermit, "if you choose to pursue the Goddess of Personal Improvement, the Goddess of Wealth will become extremely jealous, and as a result, she will pay more attention to you. In fact, the more you seek and pursue the Goddess of Personal Improvement, the Goddess of Wealth will even chase you. She will even chase after you to the point that she will constantly shower you with all the material and personal blessings you seek, simply to win your attention. Then," said the old hermit to the young lad, "the success and the position of life you desire will be yours forever."

Our human tendency is to pursue and chase after the Goddess of Wealth. Another way of looking at it is that this Goddess of Wealth can be best described as, *"What's in it for me?"* This always seems to be the most logical choice. After all, the Goddess of Wealth delivers the rewards we are seeking. Regardless of whether that reward consists of career advancement, material possessions, financial security, heart-throbbing relationships, or whatever our success priority may be at this time, it is that reward for which we are working. Although the reward of "What's in it for me?" is a necessary ingredient in our pursuit of success, it is mandatory that we must first pursue the Goddess of Personal Improvement.

Along those same lines, another way we can describe this Goddess of Personal Improvement is *"What am I able to bring to the table?"* The more we can bring to the table through our pursuit of the Goddess of Personal Improvement, the more the Goddess of Wealth will shower us with the rewards of the success we are seeking.

While this concept may seem logical, in so many instances, that is the part of the equation that we so often miss. As we will discuss in more detail shortly, it's important to understand that for every cause, there is an equal effect. Therefore, if the reward offered by the Goddess of Wealth is our desired effect, then the cause that will produce those rewards will be determined by *"What I can bring to the table?"* as a result of first pursuing the Goddess of Personal Improvement.

Regardless of how each of us may define that personal improvement, the more we pursue it and the higher the value that we can bring to the table, the faster we will reach that next plateau of the success we seek, regardless of how we may define that plateau. The more value we bring to the table, the more likely it will be that we will become our best rendition.

The Aptitude of Mindset

Brian Tracy, the legendary best-selling author, and corporate trainer observes that *"Success is as predictable as the sun rising in the East and setting in the West."* Indeed, most often success can be just that predictable. With this being the case, let's now consider a few behaviors and mindsets that successful people practice that will point us in the direction of that success.

The chances are that most everyone has at one time or another taken a personality test such as the Myers Briggs Type Indicator or the Minnesota Multiphasic Personality Inventory test. Or maybe an aptitude test for a prospective employer.

Research has shown that people who have formed a similar mindset will answer questions with similar answers, all which points to how they process their thoughts, which in the end is also a relatively good indication of what their actions will be.

In the same way, people who have achieved a high degree of sustainable success usually think from a different mindset compared to others who may fall into the category of being more mediocre in the same industry or profession.

"How" we think and process our thoughts will to a great extent determine not only what we do, but also may be a good indication as to the level of success we may obtain in the area of our endeavors.

Whatever our chosen profession, or the endeavors we may pursue, if we desire to be a success at what we do and who we are, then, as discussed earlier, not only do we need to learn *how* successful people think, but we also need to understand the premises of the *why* of their thought processes.

Notice how I said we need to learn *how* a successful person thinks, not *what* they think. There is a difference.

The *how* we think is the method by which we formulate our plans and then put those plans into action.

The *how* we think often translates into how we process the *what* we think, which ultimately can become the justification and the rationalization for not only what we do, but also why we do it.

So, with that, let's devote the rest of this chapter attempting to get into the minds of those whom society typically looks upon and considers as being successful in their respective professions and in who they are.

Let me point something out that is very important. Often, we will discover that the changes we need to make in our thinking process may not be all that dramatic. As a rule, we will often find that the slightest change will usually provide the most extraordinary results and rewards.

I'm not here to tell you that your thinking is all wrong; the chances are that it's not. What I am saying, however, is that as is the case with most all of us, sometimes even the slightest change in how we think may produce a very dramatic and positive result.

Let me use just two analogies to make my point.

When I was in my mid 20s, I decided to take up flying as a private pilot. Back then there was no such thing as a GPS. As a private pilot, learning to navigate was one of the first lessons taught. As a student, you soon learned that merely flying in a general direction can get you in real trouble. If you chart your course and it dictates that you are to fly on a course of say true North, a 0.00 compass heading, then that is the course you had better remain committed to. If you were to change your course by say only five degrees, even though you may still be flying in a Northerly direction, if you continued flying for say 100 miles, your ultimate destination would be miles and miles different from your original desired destination, had you remained on your true north heading.

Let's consider another analogy. If you're a horse racing fan, I am sure that you have seen many times when two horses who are so close as they cross the finish line that it is virtually impossible for the human eye to determine who the winner is. When this occurs, it is referred to as a "photo finish" because a photo is taken as the horses cross the finish line. From the photo that's snapped, it is often proven that the winning horse wins by mere inches, and most often, it's the nose of the two horses as they cross the finish line that measures those few inches.

Consider that at the speed the horses are running, which is generally estimated at somewhere between 50 to 55 mph, how long then does it take a horse to travel that short distance of say 1½ to 2 inches that determines the winner. The horse whose nose crosses the finish line first can sometimes earn two, three, or even four times more in winnings than the horse who comes in second place.

Consider the horse that came in second. How much of an extra effort would it have had to put forth during the ast 100 yards to make up that two inches or less? For that matter, how much would the jockey have had to adjust the horse's stride or its pace over the length of the entire race to make up that two inches? Because it failed to put forth that little extra effort, the horse that came in second went home with substantially less of the total purse than the one who came in first. Second place seldom sets the pace. Second place rarely raises the bar. Second place seldom gets highlighted in the record books.

Life is no different. Sometimes it can be the slightest change in the direction we are heading or the slightest extra effort that can make the most dramatic difference in our life. It's easy to pick up on the big things that require change; however, we can often miss those small, yet so essential, changes that often will so dramatically change the destiny of our life when we lose our focus.

3

Building Our Foundation

As I mentioned earlier, I spent a great deal of my adult life in the Real Estate Construction and Development business. When beginning a new project, once we had the building site prepared, our next primary objective was to build a solid foundation. The integrity of the foundation not only determines the integrity of the total structure but will also define the form and function that the building will take. Every time I change the direction or angle of the foundation, which will also affect the form that the building will take. As the form goes, so too will how the structure will function. For example, if the form of my building is the shape of a triangle, it will function very differently compared to a square-shaped structure. In many ways that same could be said of our life. Naturally, the integrity of the strength of our foundation is essential, but the form that our life's foundation will take will also determine how our life will function.

If our goal is to build a solid foundation to support and have a mindset that will enhance our ability to succeed in what we do and who we are, then we need to begin by looking at several necessary ingredients that must go into building that foundation.

One of these primary ingredients is having a basic understanding of just how much control we have over our lives.

It's an Inalienable Right

If we watch very much of the 24-hour news channels or even the network news, it doesn't take long before we develop the mindset that the whole world is going to hell in a handbasket. It's easy to get the impression that everything is spinning out of control and there is not a darn thing anyone can do about it.

Now, while none of us as individuals may have much control over the events in the world at large, but just because we have little or no control over the events that go on in say, North Korea, we shouldn't have that attitude about our life and our world. We just can't throw in the towel and say we also have no control over our lives. We all have a lot more control than we often want to admit. Whenever we throw in the towel, aren't we admitting defeat? And if it's not a defeat, then it's easy for it to become an excuse for not accepting the responsibility for taking the control that is available to us.

Permit me to take you through a little exercise that I often use in my seminars and retreats that will help to accentuate just how much control each of us has over our life and our future. Although you are reading this text versus hearing my voice, I think you will get the point I am attempting to make.

First, I invite you to go deep into the thoughts that are running through your mind at this specific moment. Think about the thoughts that concern you, not about this exercise, its purpose or what is to come next. Think about how your day is going today. What you have already accomplished and what lies ahead for the rest of your day.

Now I invite you to put your thoughts about your day today on hold and now shift your thoughts to the most memorable vacation you had ever had. How long ago did that vacation occur? What was it that made it memorable? Who did you share that memorable time with?

Now I invite you to shift your thoughts one more time. This time I ask that you think about the plans you have for Christmas next year. Will you be traveling for the holidays? Is the time leading up to Christmas a busy and somewhat hectic time, and do you anticipate it being the same for this one also?

OK, now it's time to gather your thoughts and come back to the here and now.

The little exercise that you just completed is an exercise that can only be done by the human species. No other created creature can do what you had just done. In the span of only a few minutes, you shifted your thoughts from the present, then to the past, then to the future, and finally back to the present again.

This little exercise is proof that we as humans can change our thoughts and what we are thinking about simply by making the decision to do so. Only we as humans have 100% control of our thinking and thought process. If we are in a bad mood, we have 100% control to change that mood by merely deciding to do so. Only we as humans have the power and ability to think about what we are thinking about. Then with a blink of the eye we can also change what it is that we are thinking about.

There is a school of psychology and psychologist who are often referred to as "Determinist." It is their theory that our personality and character is typically developed and determined because of one or more of three primary causes of which we have no control over.

The first of which is our genealogy or ancestry. For example, a determinist may say that if I'm of German descent, then my personality is one that I am stubborn, and can be very strong willed. If I'm Irish, then I have more of a free spirit and do not take life so seriously. If I'm Italian, then I'm ... If I'm African-American, then I'm ...

I'm sure you get the point. According to this line of thought if it's in my blood and engrained into my DNA, then that's who I am, and what I will become, and it's out of my control.

Accordingly, the second cause that a determinist will say that our character and personality can be determined by is that of our parents. For example, if one of my parents was abusive, then I will also be abusive. If, on the other hand they are loving, caring, and nurturing parents, then that will guarantee that I will automatically be such also.

And the third cause, according to their school of thought, is the result of our environment. This line of thinking says that if I live in a bad neighborhood or go to a lousy school and have bad teachers. Or if I have an unfair boss, or if my employees are undependable, or if my spouse just don't understand me, or I'm in a bad marriage, then it will be those events that will create the environment that can determine what my personality and character will become, and how I will form and then act upon my thoughts.

Most have heard or read about the Austrian psychologist Dr. Victor Frankl. Or maybe most will know of him more as a Holocaust Survivor and author.

While in the Nazi Concentration Camp he endured unimaginable suffering. Both of his parents and siblings were either executed or starved to death right before his eyes. His most notable work that resulted from his experience is entitled, *"Man's Search for Meaning."*

At the time of his arrest by the Nazi's, as an educated and learned psychologist, he would have been defined as a Determinist. As such he believed that we are who we are because of either our ancestors, our parents, or our environment, or a combination thereof.

Due to his dreadful experience, that belief was drastically changed. In his writings, he observed that while one's past, or even events of one's current condition and environment, can *influence* our thinking, only we as individuals, as humans who have been created in the image and likeness of our God, with the freedom of will, have total and absolute control over our thoughts and being as to who we are.

As a result of his horrific experience he observed that *"When we are no longer able to change a situation, we are challenged to change ourselves."* He further said, *"Everything can be taken from a man but one thing: The last of the human freedoms—to choose one's attitude in any given set of circumstances, to choose one's own way."*

So, as Dr. Frankl points out, we have 100% control over our thoughts, and from the thoughts that we, as individual human beings decide to have, will come the ultimate life that we will experience.

Regardless of the neighborhood I grew up in; regardless of what stupid and hurtful words a teacher may have said to me; regardless of what my parents may have done to me, for me, or with me; regardless of whatever my past may have consisted of, or the experiences I have had, I, right at this very minute, have the ability, and the God-given right and freedom to change whatever thoughts I may be having. The very thoughts of which may be holding me back from becoming my best rendition.

When you think about it, having control over our life and its destiny is a part of who we are as human beings. Our freedom of control is part of our DNA. Our forefathers stated this as a God-given inalienable right. The reason this right is held to be so sacred, and as an absolute right, all has to do with the reality of our inborn God-given purpose.

In this book, I'm not promoting religion or even a level of spirituality. What I am promoting is purpose. I'm upholding the belief that there was a purpose behind the reason for creation, and equally as important, there is purpose in and for each one of our lives.

I think it boils down to this. *Purpose* is the product of *Intelligent Intent. Intelligent Intent* results in *control,* so the more we assume our responsibility to take control of our career, our life and our destiny, the more we will fulfill our purpose, and the more we achieve our purpose, the better rendition of ourselves we will become.

It's Bigger than Just Me

To carry this idea a bit further, let's begin by considering how special and unique the creation of humanity is over that of all other created creatures.

As humans, not only were we given a mind, an intellect, and a free will, but what is just as remarkable and unique is that each one of us have also been entrusted with our own specific talents and abilities. No other created creature can even come close to claiming the same level of talents and abilities that we humans possess. To go one step further, what is just as remarkable, believe it or not, is that our talents and abilities were entrusted to us not only for our personal use and gain, but even more so for the continued positive growth and the good of all of society.

For example, lumberjacks use their personal and individual talents and skills to cut and harvest the trees. Truck drivers use their talents and skills to deliver the harvested trees to the paper mill. The workers at the mill use their talents and skills to produce the paper that is delivered to the engineer, who in turn designs even more efficient ways in which the trees can be harvested. The trucks can become more dependable, and the paper mill can become safer and more productive.

In each of these examples, does each worker earn a wage for their own personal gain? Absolutely! That's called the fruits of their labor, yet it takes the work and skill of everyone's unique talents and abilities to make this a better world for us all.

Because this is such an important issue for us to understand, permit me to put another little twist on it so I can drive this point home with a more convincing argument.

As I have just stated, the talents and abilities that we possess were entrusted to us not only for our personal use and gain but even more so for the continued growth and the good of all of society. I recognize that this statement may for some appear to be counter cultural. For a variety of reasons many today have become too inwardly focused and have evolved into a "what's in it for me" or just as bad, "it's all about me" society.

Therefore, when it is suggested that our talents and ability were entrusted to us, not only for our use and gain but *even more so* for the continued growth and good of all of society, again, this statement can seem almost counter-cultural. Let me assure you; this is not the case. The only way we can become the best version of ourselves, and gain the most for ourselves, is when this statement is fully embraced as a focus on all that we do and all of who we are.

Consider this: Picture in your mind the most successful physician you know. Now for this physician, I am not defining success based on the size of her bank account, the size of her home, or the car she drives. Instead, I am referring to the success she enjoys with the high quality of her reputation that she has as a physician. I am defining her success based on her ability to accurately diagnose a problematic case, and her ability to develop a successful treatment plan. Her success due to her ability to show empathy to her patients with a professional, yet caring degree of sincerity. Her success due to her ability to effectively communicate with her patients, her staff, and colleagues.

Now I would challenge you to consider every one of your physicians' success attributes carefully. As you do so, I am sure you can identify that her success as a physician is the result of her using the talents and abilities she has been entrusted with for the good of her patients. The greater she develops her talents and abilities for this purpose, the more success she will enjoy as a physician.

Does she also enjoy what can be often described as substantial financial rewards? Absolutely. Do her financial rewards enable her to live in a beautiful home and drive a nice car? Absolutely. As a physician, is she in demand and does she find her waiting room filled every day? Absolutely. Does she also enjoy the respect of her patients and piers? Yes, without a doubt. But be assured that her financial rewards, her beautiful home, her nice car, and the respect she has earned would all be substantially decreased, if not even eliminated, if her only focus was on "what's in it for me." Her real success as a physician can be attributed to her first developing her talents and abilities to their very best, and then by using her developed talents and abilities for the continued positive good of her patients (i.e. her community).

Now the argument can naturally be made that there are some physicians, as there are those in every profession, who are out for themselves only, with little concern as to what they can bring to the table for the good of others. And while that may be true, let's not forget that the total focus of this book is on becoming our best rendition, and that will never happen when our focus is primarily on taking short cuts to get where we want to go.

The physician in our example above didn't take shortcuts. She did her level best, first to develop her God-given talents, and then focused on developing a personality and work ethic that would bring the absolute most to the table for her patients, her staff, and her colleagues.

That same scenario can be applied to virtually every successful person, regardless of their profession. Zig Ziglar often said that *"you can get anything out of life that you want as long as you help enough other people get what they want."*

If we study the lives of most successful people throughout history, in virtually every case, those who enjoyed true and sustaining success are those who used their talents and abilities to fulfill a need in society. Regardless of whether it's in science, medicine, technology, business, education, one of the many trades, or whatever discipline you can name, those who enjoy real and lasting success are always those who first have a focus on developing their talents and abilities to the maximum, and then using them to answer the unmet needs of those they serve; in other words, "for the continued positive growth and good of society."

It's easy to point to some of the hugely successful and notable high-tec inventers and gurus of today and demonstrate how, due to their fulfilling an unmet need, society rewarded them with the financial success and notoriety they enjoy, and that's true.

But so often we fail to look right in our hometown communities, and consider those who are truly serving unmet needs every day, and how by serving those unmet needs, they also are achieving a level of success that enables them to become their best rendition.

Think of your local pharmacist who meticulously counts every pill, and then checks and rechecks the prescription. Fulfilling the needs of those she serves without cutting corners.... Becoming her best rendition.

Consider the carpenter who takes pride in the quality of his craftsmanship, and even though the money he earns will be the same, he takes the extra time necessary to deliver a product to his customer that he is willing to put his name on—fulfilling the needs of those he serves without cutting corners; becoming his best rendition.

Now let's bring that home for a bit. I would challenge you to spend whatever time you need to reflect on the talents and abilities that have been explicitly entrusted to you. Because our talents and abilities play such a critical role in how we define ourselves, this is an essential exercise. So again, take as much time as you need to consider your answer very carefully and honestly. This isn't a time to be shy or even to display an unhealthy dose of humility. Instead, this is a time to take an honest and sincere inventory of your true talents and abilities.

Consider your talents and abilities that involve your personality:

✓ Are you a good listener?
✓ Can you show compassion without pity?
✓ Do family, friends, and maybe even co-workers seek advice from you?
✓ Can you maintain a level head during times of crises?
✓ Do others consider you as an understanding and patient person?
✓ Are you more often considered as a leader or a solid team player, or do you think of yourself as more of an independent who does your own thing, in your own way?
✓ Do you tend to look at the glass as being half full or half empty?
✓ In your family, your social circle, or your professional arena, would others describe your personality as one who searches for and promotes opportunity for improvement of the common good?
✓ Can you think things through?
✓ Are you a quick study and learn things quickly?

- ✓ What other personality traits do you have that can be described as either a talent, ability or a trait that can enhance who you are to become your best?
- ✓ Now how about your talents and abilities that involve your skills?
- ✓ Do you consider yourself as having a high level of energy?
- ✓ Are you mechanically inclined?
- ✓ Do you have exceptional hand-eye coordination?
- ✓ Does your comprehension of the sciences come easily to you?
- ✓ For you, how would you describe a good day's work, and what skills did you employ to accomplish your objectives?
- ✓ What skills do you employ that provides you the greatest satisfaction and fulfillment?
- ✓ What skills do you employ that fulfills the unmet needs of others?

Of course, our list of examples of our talents and abilities that include both our personality and our skills can also include other good examples, but I think you get the point of this exercise. Because this is essential, I encourage you to take as much time as necessary so that your inventory is as accurate as possible. Do not underestimate how much you have to offer, and how many unmet needs that you can fulfill.

As you contemplate your overall inventory, I invite you to list them in the space provided below.

My talents and abilities relating to my personality:

1_____

2._____

3._____

4. _____

5._____

My talents and abilities relating to my skills:

1._____

2._____

3._____

4. _____

5._____

As you listed your talents and abilities above, if more than five in each basic category comes to mine, no problem! Write everything that comes to your mind. If, however, you can't complete the full list of five in each, that's not a problem either. It's far more important to have an honest and accurate inventory than it is to enumerate your list.

Once your inventory is complete, I would now challenge you to review each of your listed talents and abilities carefully. The chances are that there will be one, two, or maybe even three that will float to the top and shine more than all the others. It will be these talents and abilities that have highlighted themselves as being the most predominant that you will want to focus on the most. As you do so ask yourself several key questions:

✓ How have I developed these key talents and abilities to their greatest potential?
✓ What actions do I need to take and what commitments must I make to myself to further develop these key talents and abilities?
✓ How can these talents and abilities be used to serve my clients, customers, students, patients, employer, employees, or any other title you may give to those I serve?
✓ In what way do I use my talents and abilities to fulfill the unmet

needs of those I serve, and how can I be of further service?

✓ By developing these to their maximum potential and then using them in the best way I can, how, by answering the needs of others who I serve, will it also lead me to the desired destination of my life and career?

With the entrustment of our specific talents and abilities, we each have a responsibility to society to develop them to their maximum potential, and to use them in the best way we can. Until we develop them to their utmost, we will never reach our maximum potential and thus become our best rendition.

It is only when we strive to become our best so to reach our maximum potential that we can hope to bring the real value of what we have to offer to the table.

Now while studies and research validate this mindset, we don't need to rely on formal studies for validation. All we need to do is consider all the successful people we know or know about who are doing just that.

Regardless of the profession, position, race, color, creed, intellect, or education, almost without exception, we will discover that because successful people approached life with a desire and determination to build that better mousetrap that can and will fulfill an unmet need, they therefore approach life with an *expectation of success.*

Earlier in Chapter one, you were invited to think about four successful people. You named a politician, a spiritual leader, a sports figure, and a businessperson. Each was someone you had labeled as a success. Now I would challenge you also to take a minute to analyze the specific need of society that each had filled, and how they were able to do it better than most of their peers.

Now take a moment to review the area of success you had

written earlier that is important to you. As you do so, I would ask you to consider the reality that you not only have the opportunity to achieve this level of success, but you also have a responsibility to your community to reach the highest level of success possible.

The fact is, each one of us has an incredible power within our being. Research is continuously concluding that never, at any time in history, have we come so close to understanding our true nature and the incredible power that each of us has within ourselves that can determine our destiny.

Every day we are learning more and more about our innate capacity to shape our lives and our ability to achieve the outcome that we desire.

To validate this point, I would like to cite just two of several studies conducted on this subject:

For the first. On September 16, 2015, Dr Bobby Hoffman published an article in which he cited: *"The instrumental forces that drive and directs our behaviors are based on a series of tacit beliefs that we have about ourselves. In aggregate these self-beliefs determine the direction and intensity of our motivational actions. Our beliefs determine what we do, how we do it, and how we see our accomplishments in relation to the rest of the world."* Dr. Hoffman goes on to say, *"Self-beliefs are so powerful that the evaluations will strongly influence the careers we seek, the relationships we pursue, and ultimately what we do or do not accomplish in life."* [1]

Another study was conducted by Stanford Psychologist Carol Dweck and published in her book entitled *Mindset: The New Psychology of Success*. In her work she delved into the reality of the power of our

---

[1] Educational Psychologist Dr. Bobby Hoffman, Associate Professor in the School of Teaching, Learning, and Leadership at the University of Central Florida. Published by the Elsevier's Academic Press. September 16, 2015

beliefs and how by changing the simplest of both our conscious and unconscious thoughts can have a profound impact on nearly every aspect of our lives.

Dr. Dweck writes: *"For twenty years, my research has shown that the view you adopt for yourself affects the way you lead your life. It can determine whether you become the person you want to be and whether you accomplish the things you value. How does this happen? How can a simple belief have the power to transform your psychology and, as a result, your life?*

She further states, *"Believing that your qualities are carved in stone—the fixed mindset—creates an urgency to prove yourself over and over. If you have only a certain amount of intelligence, a certain personality, and a certain moral character—well, then you'd better prove that you have a healthy dose of them. It simply wouldn't do to look or feel deficient in these most basic characteristics."*

She then goes on to say, *"I've seen so many people with this one consuming goal of proving themselves—in the classroom, in their careers, and their relationships. Every situation calls for a confirmation of their intelligence, personality, or character. Every situation is evaluated: Will I succeed or fail? Will I look smart or dumb? Will I be accepted or rejected? Will I feel like a winner or a loser?*

But she continues, *"There's another mindset in which these traits are not simply a hand you're dealt and have to live with, always trying to convince yourself and others that you have a royal flush when you're secretly worried it's a pair of tens. In this mindset, the hand you're dealt is just the starting point for development. This growth mindset is based on the belief that your basic qualities are things you can cultivate through your efforts. Although people may differ in every which way —in their initial talents and aptitudes, interests, or temperaments— everyone can change and grow through application and experience.*

Do people with this mindset believe that anyone can be anything, that anyone with proper motivation or education can become Einstein or Beethoven? No, but they believe that a person's true potential is unknown (and unknowable); that it's impossible to foresee what can be accomplished with years of passion, toil, and training." [2]

Most current studies available can be very compelling. We only need to choose to access this power that lies w thin us; this power that is part of our DNA; this power that has been entrusted to us, which we have been charged with the responsibility to develop and use and become the best rendition of ourselves that we can become.

To maximize our success and the growth we can enjoy, regardless of the endeavors that may be our focus, we need to develop the mindset of those who are successful. By doing so, we can also master that power that lies deep within ourselves. If we fail to tap into this incredible power, life will just pass us by, and we will miss out on, or better yet, cheat ourselves out of so many of the amenities and rewards that life has to offer.

Only when we tap into this power of our natural inner being can we transform our lives from ordinary to the extraordinary. We move from being the person who plugs along day in and day out, to earning the real rewards that life makes available to us all. Without any doubt, we can change for the better the degree of satisfaction and fulfillment we obtain from our journey.

What we have been given, is the greatest do-it-yourself kit ever devised. Regardless of the endeavor we may be seeking, whether it involves our career, our finances, our relationships, or whatever. For us to become the best rendition of ourselves, it is our responsibility to dig deep so as to recognize our talents, our abilities, our personalities,

[2] *Mindset: The New Psychology of Success by* Carrol S. Dweck, Ballantine Books, ©2006, 2016

and all the uniqueness that creation has entrusted to us, and then use that power to develop all the potential we have, so as to become all that we can become for both ourselves and our community.

For a more in-depth discussion on our personal responsibility to better utilize that great power that lies within us, let us now turn to another essential ingredient that goes into building our foundation for success.

4

Our Connectedness

As humans, because we live and work together as a community, to one degree or another we are all connected. This connectedness not only has a significant impact as to what I do with my life but will also have an influence on you, and vice versa.

Understanding the reality of this connectedness is an important part, both of our foundation and our understanding as to why society has both a desire, and yes, even a need for us to succeed. To better grasp this concept let's turn for a minute to science.

If you recall from elementary school, one of the first lessons in science that we were taught was that of an atom. We were informed that the atom is the smallest form of all matter and that it is made up of total energy. This energy is produced by a cluster of neutrons and protons that make up the nucleus of the atom. Swirling around its nucleus (or core) are electrons that are moving at the speed of light—186,000 miles per second.

Because the atom is the foundation of everything, and because it's 100% energy, every object and every being are also made up of this same 100% energy.

We know that this energy produces waves that are constantly vibrating and pulsating. We were taught that everything that we can see or touch, or even the particles that we can smell, are continually vibrating and pulsating this energy.

This is also true of our bodies since they're also made up of atoms and energy. The fact is that we are merely bundles of this 100% energy. Because of this energy and the energy that is produced and pulsating from everything around us, science also tells us that to one degree or another we are all connected through this ever-present and ever-pulsating energy.

At first, you may think that this idea of us being connected is a bit of science fiction. However, our everyday experiences tell us of its reality.

Let's use a visual analogy of a large swimming pool, and let's assume that our pool is the size of a large public municipal pool. Now in that pool say there are only six to eight people. Each person is in various places throughout the pool, and at varying distance from each other, and then you jump in.

Even though no one in the pool is touching another person and even a bit of a distance from each other, because of the molecules of the water you could say that you are all physically connected.

Now if you question the degree by how much you are connected, I would challenge you to throw an electrical wire into the water and see how connected you each are! Although I naturally would not recommend you do this, but if you did, you would soon discover that within a blink of the eye, everyone in the pool would experience an electrical shock.

Because we can see and feel the presence of the physical matter of the water, it's relatively easy for us to understand this connectedness. In a somewhat similar manner, we are all connected via this pulsating and vibrating electrical energy that makes up the universe that we live in.

As a result of that connectedness, not only are we influenced by others and the circumstances around us, but in turn, we also have an impact on the lives of others in the world we live in.

Let's consider a few everyday examples of how we are connected by this vibrating energy that surrounds us and the impact it has on us.

Have you ever been in a room alone and suddenly felt that you were no longer alone? You turn around, and sure enough, you discover someone standing there!

Or, how often has it happened that you were in a crowd at some gathering and you get this feeling that someone is focused or directing his or her attention toward you? As you scan the room, sure enough, you find that person standing across the hall from you, and your eyes meet for no apparent reason. At that split second you both felt an unexplained connection that drew your eyes toward one another. How often don't we hear lovers tell the story of how they met, and it was in just this manner. For some unexplainable reason their eyes met, and they felt an immediate connection.

When I'm talking about this connectedness, I am not referring to some telepathic powers of someone trying to manipulate or control the thoughts of someone else. Naturally, as we have made it very clear earlier, both you and the other person have the freedom to remain connected to another conversation or objective you may be involved in, and therefore, ignore those feelings. Also, because both you and the other person have absolute control over your thoughts, even if that connected thought does come to you, you each maintain the power to change that thought by merely making the decision to do so.

Depending on how absorbed you are in what you are currently doing or with whom you are engaged, you may not even pick up on the vibrations you are receiving, but that doesn't mean that they are not there.

By now you're probably asking just how all this talk about the structure of an atom and how we are all connected through this electrical force of energy has anything to do with our ability to control the *destiny* of either our career or our life?

To oversimplify the answer, because of our connectedness and the positive or negative effect that we have on each other, it's critical that we can take control of those forces that *are not* in your best interest, and to welcome and embrace all those forces that *are*.

Going back again to the analogy of the swimming pool. Consider the ripple effect that occurs when I throw a pebble into the water. We are aware of the fact that the larger the stone, the more pronounced the ripple will be, and the greater outreach it will have.

So too, the higher the potential impact that others may have on us, or us on them, the higher the need exists to maintain control.

As an example, think of the adverse and energy-draining impact it can have on our entire nation when we experience the devastation of a mass shooting, a terrorist attack, or a catastrophic natural disaster.

Unfortunately, there has been way too many of these instances, and most all of us can site that disastrous event that may have had the most devastating impact on our life.

One instance that I can still vividly recall is the energy draining impact that 9/11 had on me. This was not only an attack on our homeland by a foreign group, but it went beyond what we would consider as a remote possibility. The reality of it was almost beyond comprehension. I, like many of you, can remember how glued we were to the TV as every story was run repeatedly. For days, this story and its latest developments occupied virtually 100% of the airwaves. I can remember the subdued mood of everyone at the office while the story was unraveling. It occupied the mind of everyone you spoke with. No one felt they had the right or permission to smile, to laugh, or have a good time. It reminded me of the feeling and an atmosphere a person can experience when in a funeral home. But then again, why shouldn't it, after all the entire nation was in mourning.

After the third day of this, I remember coming home from work and telling my wife that we were turning the TV off, and for a change of mood and our psyche we were going out for dinner. But there was no escape. The mood and temperament of those at the restaurant were just as subdued as everywhere else. Only occasionally would you hear a peal of laughter, but even then, it was in a low tone and short lived.

Without a doubt, we were all connected. Even though none of us were anywhere near the sites of any of the attacks, the adverse ripple effect impacted us all.

On the reverse side, think of how good you feel and how energized you become when your favorite sports team wins that championship or other notable accomplishments.

Going back again to the 9/11 experience, out of respect for the 3,000 people who had lost their lives in this tragedy, then Baseball Commissioner Bud Selig had decided to halt all games throughout the country; first for a day, then three days, and ultimately six days. For the City of New York, baseball did not resume until September 21, a full ten days after. But it was time for both the nation and the city of New York to permit themselves to laugh again. It was not with a feeling or attitude of trying to forget or even putting this behind us, but rather with the determination that although we as a nation had suffered a devastating blow, we were by no means down for the count.

On that day of September 21st in New York's Shea Stadium, the New York Mets and the Atlanta Braves joined as one. During an emotional pre-game ceremony, Diana Ross sang a very heart felt "God Bless America" with Mayor Rudy Giuliana giving a "Thumbs Up" from his seat, America began its healing process. America began to reenergize. Once again proof that we are indeed connected.

Whether the effect of the event is positive or negative, the impact that we experience will be in direct proportion to how close we are related to the event. The closer the relationship, the bigger the pebble becomes, which results in a more significant impact and affect the ripple has on us

Once we acknowledge and understand the degree to which our connectedness affects us, it then gives us a better understanding of the need we have to maintain control over our thoughts, actions, and attitudes when that ripple hits us.

For example, once I understand that I have no control over the amount of loyalty of a customer or client, it then helps me to control my thoughts, attitude, and even actions when that loyalty is not there. After all, how can I possibly take the actions or attitudes of others personally when it is something that is undeniably out of my control?

Once I understand that I have no control over how a fellow employee, an acquaintance, or even a friend or family member may treat me, it then helps me to understand the responsibility I have to control my thoughts, attitude, and actions in relation to how I may, in turn, react to them.

We tend to lose control of situations when we react to them. We are much more likely to maintain control when we respond to the situation. When we only react to what is going on in our life, we seldom think it through as we should. When we respond, however, we are more apt to stop to consider the big picture and what we can do to keep the situation under the control needed for the outcome to be more positive.

Because animals function only from instinct, they can only react to the immediate situation. We humans, on the other hand, have the intellect of a mind with the power to change our thoughts at will in the direction we choose, and as such, we can make the choice as to if we react out of simple instinct like an animal or if we respond by using the intellect of our mind. Whenever we lose control or do not assume the responsibility to take control, it is then that we relinquish our control and allow the circumstances to control us. I would imagine that most of us can think of situations in our lives when we were guilty of just that.

I can remember an incident when I was working with our Chamber of Commerce's Economic Development Group. My company, along with several other developers, were invited to submit proposals for a design/build facility for a prospective firm looking to expand into our community. It was a rather large facility with numerous specialty issues that related to their specific needs. The design team that I assembled worked diligently with the prospect's engineers to make sure we had an accurate understanding of their needs. We spent close to a month of burning the midnight candle in our effort to land this project.

Then came the day for the presentations. The administration and engineers of the prospect gathered in a large conference room at the Chamber of Commerce office and each developer was provided an opportunity to deliver their proposal. We were told at the time that all proposals would be seriously considered, and we would be notified of who they selected within five days.

My entire team felt our presentation went flawlessly. We felt we met their every need and answered every question they asked during our presentation. In the days that followed, their engineers had sent us several follow up questions. This added to our optimism. Five days went past and no answer. Then the sixth day and still no answer. Finally, on the seventh day the decision was made, and sad to say the answer was not what we had hoped it would be. The client selected a competitor.

To make things even worse, I stewed about this loss for the next week or so. Now it's not unusual to mourn a loss, but this went beyond simple grief. While over the years I have become accustomed to not winning every proposal or bid, but for some reason this one was different. In retrospect I think it was different due to the community involvement and the coverage this project was given by the local press.

I agonized over this to the point that I interpreted myself and my team as being the losers of the game. While it was true that we lost the deal to a competitor, because I did not immediately regain control, and because I failed to make the decision to change my attitude of what I was dwelling on, what became the most devastating for me was that during the period that I was having my little pity-party, the circumstances of the loss had taken control of my brain and attitude and it continued to reaffirm that I was a loser. This was a classic case in which losing to the competition was the least costly for me. Until I was able to regain control and begin to refocus on generating positive magnetic energy, I would continue to block any positive inspiration that may shine a light of future opportunities that may be even bigger and better than the one I was grieving. Most of us have been in similar situations. The question is whether you think you reacted to the situation or did you respond to it?

Parents can often find themselves in a state of guilt when a child they feel responsible for makes a bad choice in life that can result in a life-impacting consequence. Parent must accept the reality that once that child has reached the age of adult reasoning, they are only responsible for controlling their own emotions and feelings and have little or no control over the final actions of a child. Once again, do we react to what the child did, or did we respond?

A married person who feels betrayed by his or her spouse can only control his or her actions, thoughts, and emotions and not those of their spouse. In this situation, when that self-control is not accepted, it is then that the power of our thoughts, feelings, and emotions, can be relinquished to the other person. Healing can only occur once responsibility for control is accepted and regained. Once again, do we react, or do we respond?

In our professional lives, how many situations can we think about when the outcome of an event could have been totally different if only those involved would have responded instead of reacting?

There is an old American Indian saying that says, *"If a snake bites you, chasing after the snake will not get rid of the poison, it will only make it go through the body faster."* But how often don't we tend to do just that? We chase after and even hold onto that snake that bit us.

Over the years I have encountered countless people from employees, business associates, friends, family, or folks I dealt with due to my work with the Church, who have experienced the heartbreaking transition of life due to the devastation of a divorce. Typically, the more confrontational the separation, the deeper the wounds. The deeper the wounds, the more poison that has been inflicted, and the more difficult it is to let go. Regardless of how undeserving a person may be, or how justifiable the anger may be, the transition to a life with a new normal will never occur until one or both parties let go.

Regardless if it's a broken relationship, a lost sale, the disloyalty of an employer or an employee, or whatever the case in life would be, the sooner we learn to let go of whatever it was that inflicted the poison, and not chase after it, the sooner we can address the poison and make the successful transition of getting beyond it. Until we elect to make the conscious decision to address the poison and not concern ourselves with the snake, the sooner the healing can begin.

I would again like to remind you of the words of wisdom from Victor Frankl when he said, *"When we are no longer able to change a situation, we are challenged to change ourselves."* He continued, *"Everything can be taken from a man but one thing: The last of the human freedoms— to choose one's attitude in any given set of circumstances, to choose one's own way."* This, my friends, is the true meaning of responding to life rather than reacting to it.

The Law of Cause and Effect

Because we are all connected through this force of energy that surrounds us, as well as the importance that our thoughts and emotions play in determining who we are and what we become, by far, one of the important laws and principles of the universe that we need to understand is the *Law of Cause and Effect*.

Having a basic understanding of this law is another primary ingredient that forms the foundation of who we are and is an absolute necessity and critical aspect in maintaining control in our life.

This law of cause and effect states that *everything is produced as a direct result of a cause, and from that cause, there will always be a direct and corresponding effect.*

For almost every positive cause you will find a corresponding positive effect or result. Likewise, almost every negative cause will end with a corresponding negative effect or results.

Only by maintaining positive control with an appropriate response, regardless of the actions, thoughts, or attitudes of others, can we be the catalyst that will produce a positive effect or results in our lives.

Understanding this fundamental and essential law of cause and effect helps us to realize the critical role that our attitudes, beliefs, behaviors, decisions, and actions will play in both who we are today and who we will become.

By maintaining control and responding to the events of life, we control the cause that will produce the effect. When we only react, often the resulting effect we cause will be neither positive nor productive.

Our understanding of this basic, but important, principle brings into focus just how much control we elect to take over all aspects of our life, and the destiny as to where our life may lead us. This control can only happen when we make the conscious decision to respond to the events of life, instead of reacting out of impulse.

This is another critical mindset that successful people have adopted as part of their foundation. Successful individuals are fully aware that their mindset in relation to how they look at life and the world around them, will to a great extent govern their actions. Consequently, it will be their attitudes and actions that will produce the "cause" that will determine the inevitable outcome as to what and who they become, in their career, their life, or their destiny. Simply out, we often have the ability to produce the cause that will determine the effect.

5

Our Magnetic Energy

Let's now take this law of cause and effect one step further. Quantum physics tells us that because of this bundle of 100% pulsating energy we are made of, our body radiates a field of electrical energy.

This concept may seem foreign to you, but I'm sure you're aware of several medical testing procedures that rely on this electrical energy that's produced by our body.

One such test is known as an EEG, which is an acronym for electroencephalogram, which measures our electrical brain waves.

Another medical test most of us are familiar with is known by the acronym EKG, which stands for electrocardiogram, a test that measures the electrical impulses created by our heart.

Also, if your heart stops, how do doctors attempt to restart it? They give it a boost of elecrical energy using an electrical defibrillator.

Those are just a few of the many instances where medical science has validated the fact that our bodies are a powerhouse of electrical energy.

Because we generate this energy, we radiate an incredible power of attraction. This power of attraction is created through the Positive Thinking that will attract to us all the thoughts, ideas, and answers we are seeking to fulfill our hopes, dreams, goals, and the objectives we desire to accomplish, so we can become the very best rendition of ourselves. This incredible asset that is attracted and drawn to us is the incredible gift that we humans possess and is identified as "inspiration."

So, we have two critical initial components necessary for us to become the best of ourselves that we were created to be. One is the Power of Positive Thinking, and the other is Inspiration. Let's first address the issue of the Power of Positive Thinking.

During the last 200 years, there have been countless books written about the Power of Positive Thinking. Today there is no shortage of motivational talks and seminars that promote its importance, and without any question, I am a strong proponent of it. But Positive Thinking is only one of the essential components in the equation for us to become our best rendition.

I am not of the school that believes that Positive Thinking alone will provide the answer to every situation. However, I do strongly believe that without the critical ingredient of a positive outlook and attitude, one has no chance for positive inspiration to come your way, much less for any positive resolution.

Permit me to use this example to make my point. After I retired from business, I found myself without a purpose, or reason to get out of bed in the morning. I was in an "existence" mode only and I absolutely hated it. To resolve that feeling I tried to immerse myself by working with the church and involved in community volunteer work. I found my life to be quite busy, and of course, whenever you are touching the lives of others, it naturally provides a feeling of satisfaction, yet I had the feeling that I was being called to a different direction in life.

I finally figured out that for much of my life, I had been in high-stress positions. Most every day my adrenalin was pumping at full force. Now that I was retired, this was not the case. My kids have said that I'm an adrenalin junkie, and to some extent maybe they are right. I needed to do something that would get my blood pumping, of which would once again give me the focus and purpose in life I felt I was missing.

One day after visiting a friend who was a patient at one of our regional hospitals, I ran into one of the directors whom I knew, and we began to talk. To fast forward toward the point of this story, three months later I joined their chaplaincy staff and ultimately became dual certified by the American Institute of Health Care Professionals as a Thanatologist and Grief Counselor, with an emphasis on anticipatory grief.

Now to my point: As I already stated, I am not of the position that positive thinking alone will resolve every problem or provide every answer. As an example, for a patient who is suffering from a Stage Four cancer, the chances are that Positive Thinking *alone* will not provide the cure. However, I am convinced that without Positive Thinking and a positive outlook and attitude, there is little chance for any positive outcome, regardless of how it may be described.

During my short five-year tenure at the hospital, seldom would a day go past that I could not validate examples of how the quality of life was substantially enhanced by patients who displayed a positive demeanor versus the ones who became negative, depressed, angry and gave up all hope. Most Doctors will confirm that medicine, procedures and treatments are more apt to be effective and do their intended job with a patient who has a positive outlook versus someone who is negative. I can verify that the quality of life they experienced during their journey was always substantially higher.

In an article posted on January 25, 2017, by Jane Ashley, who interviewed cancer survivor Elizabeth Edwards who said it best, *"A positive attitude is not going to save you. What it's going to do is, every day, between now and the day you die, whether that's a short time from now or a long time from now, that every day, you're going to actually live."* [3]

From my viewpoint, that alone should be considered as a very positive outcome.

So yes, the power of Positive Thinking is a vital ingredient. But we cannot rely on Positive Thinking alone. The problem that can arise when Positive Thinking is our only ingredient is that it most often turns into only "wishful" thinking, and as we all know very well, wishing alone will not accomplish anything.

True Positive Thinking is far more than the fired up, a go-get-'em feeling we get from a 30-minute motivational talk. Although Positive Thinking can and will make us *feel* better compared to having a negative or defeatist attitude, true positive thinking is much more than a feeling. True positive thinking is more than the mood one may be in. It's how we chose to experience life and view the world around us. True positive thinking does not come and go depending on the situation or some outwardly produced motivation; instead, it's a part of who we are. It's a recognizable part of our personality.

For Positive Thinking to have its most significant power, it is imperative that we first employ the primary foundational blocks

---

[3] https://www.philly.com/philly/health/a-cancer-survivor-why-positive-thinking-really-matters-20170725.html

consisting of *Faith*, *Trust*, and *Confidence*.

Let's begin with our first foundational block, which is Faith.

Faith is the state of mind of that which we hold to be true. Faith is having a clear understanding of who we are, combined with the assurance in our ability to use the talents that were entrusted to us to become the best of ourselves. The Bible says that with Faith we can move mountains, but without faith, we can do nothing. As it applies to Positive Thinking, without a solid faith in ourselves and our ability to improve our stance in life to become our best, Positive Thinking is reduced to wishful thinking that comes and goes with the latest feel-good post we may read on Facebook.

That brings us to Trust, which consists of the essence of Faith. Rather, I should say that Trust is comprised of the depth of the Faith we have in ourselves and the talents that we were entrusted with to become our best rendition. The deeper our faith, the stronger our trust.

Our final foundational block for Positive Thinking is Confidence. This embodies the depth of our Faith and the strength of our Trust. When combined, Faith, Trust, and Confidence provide the catalyst that makes our Positive Thinking a powerful force of attraction.

Only we as individuals can determine what the real power of our Positive Thinking will generate for us in our life. Every day we have the ability, and yes even the responsibility, to make the conscious decision to have either a positive attitude and outlook, or whether we will choose to be negative or pessimistic as to how we see ourselves and the world. These daily decisions become the building blocks of the foundation of the person we become.

As I have already stated, I do not believe that Positive Thinking alone can be the answer to all things. However, when our Positive Thinking is anchored in the foundation of Faith, Trust, and Confidence, it is then that we begin a new game in an entirely new arena.

I'd like to again refer to my tenure as a Thanatologist working in the Cancer Center. On numerous occasions I had patients who were involved in Clinical Trials. As you may be aware, these trials are conducted to test the clinical outcome of new drugs. The trials involve patients who volunteer for the test. A percentage of them receive the new drug that is being tested, while the remainder are given a Placebo, which could consist of anything from a sugar pill to a simple vitamin. In each case, the trial is conducted under a double-blind study in which neither the patient nor their physician is aware of the actual treatment being received. It's common knowledge that a percentage of the patients receiving the placebo also experienced healing.

This intrigued me, so I did a little digging into the subject. I discovered numerous scientific-based studies that have been conducted to verify the outcome of what is often described as the "Placebo Effect."

As it relates to our discussion here, an article was published by the *Harvard Magazine* in 2013 by Cara Feinberg, an Associate Professor of Medicine. In this article, it stated that he and colleagues from several Harvard-affiliated hospitals created the Program in Placebo Studies and the Therapeutic Encounter (PiPS), which was headquartered at Beth Israel Deaconess Medical Center, a world-class teaching hospital of Harvard Medical School in Boston, Massachusetts. The article went on to say, "researchers *have* found that placebo treatments— interventions with no active drug ingredients—can stimulate real physiological responses, from changes in heart rate and blood pressure to chemical activity in the brain, in cases involving pain, depression, anxiety, fatigue, and even some symptoms of Parkinson's."

As interesting as that may be, he went on to say, "the patients who experienced the greatest relief were those who received the most care. In an age of rushed doctor's visits and packed waiting rooms, it was the first study to show a "dose-dependent response" for a placebo: the more care people got—even if it was fake—the better they tended to fare."[4]

I think the findings by Feinberg and his group are a good indication that when Positive Thinking is rooted in the foundation of Faith, Trust, and Confidence that it can indeed move mountains.

As impressive as that is, what is just as remarkable, and has the same ability to move mountains, is when our Positive Thinking is firmly anchored on its foundation of Faith, Trust, and Confidence, it then becomes the incubator that will create the environment that will also attract our second critical ingredient necessary for us to become our best. That second, and very powerful ingredient is Inspiration.

Seldom do we recognize or even appreciate the power and value of Inspiration. So often we take for granted and discard the creative Inspirational thoughts and ideas that are attracted to us.

Consider this: Every masterpiece of art began with an inspiration. Before the artist even picked up that brush, he had a mental picture of the finished product. That's positive inspiration; and that inspiration came because of the degree of faith, trust and confidence he had in his ability to produce his inspired mental picture.

The internet and the various social media outlets all became a reality because of an inspiration. Not only was the initial concept an inspiration, but so was all the hurdles along the way before it became a reality. Even though at first it may have been considered as science fiction from Hollywood, because of the degree of faith, trust, and confidence each inventor and developer had in their ability to bring their dreams to reality, their positive thinking provided the inspiration

---

[4] https://harvardmagazine.com/2013/01/the-placebo-phenomenon

needed for each step along the way.

Without any doubt, the evidence is irrefutable—nothing good, nothing extraordinary, nothing of value, nothing that has ever resulted in making our world a better place to live has ever come about that was not the result of positive Inspiration. Positive Inspiration that was attracted to someone as a result of their Positive Thinking that was anchored in a foundation of Faith, Trust, and Confidence.

The word inspiration is derived from the word Inspire, of which from its Latin root means "in-spirit." Therefore, the basic definition of inspiration is *"to influence, move, or be guided by the divine or supernatural.* Another common definition says it means *"to breathe into"*

Every major religion throughout recorded history has recognized the power of Inspiration, and how mountains can be moved, and entire civilizations can be advanced. Regardless if you are of the belief that our Inspirational thoughts are the result of a gift of Divine Intervention, as most do, or if you believe they're the results of a chemical reaction in the brain, does not change the fact that our Inspirational thoughts, when acted upon can change our life and the world we live in.

When generated from the fuel that procuces the power of Positive Thinking, we open our minds to accept the Inspiration that will guide us toward the answers we seek to accomplish what we had never thought possible.

Unlike Positive Thinking, of which we have total control as to if we will engage it or not, Inspiration on the other hand, is totally out of our control as to the "when or how" it will come to us. By its very nature, we cannot demand when or how we will receive it or what its message will be. The "when and how" of inspiration cannot be forced, nor is it a matter of our human free will. But that does not mean that we are a simple spectator. Although we may not have the control as to the "when, how, or what," we do have full responsibility and the ability to generate what is necessary that will determine the "if" it will be attracted to us. The major factor that determines that "if" will be the product of the decision we make as to the degree of Positive Thinking we elect to generate that is grounded in the foundation of Faith, Trust, and Confidence.

While Positive Thinking provides an atmosphere that will deliver the power of attraction for Inspiration to present itself. Negative thinking, on the other hand, will choke out and block all possibility for the attraction of positive Inspiration.

So, the "if" we receive the power of Inspiration is totally within our control based the positive or negative mindset we elect to generate. In essence, one could say that because of the power of magnetic attraction, our Positive Thinking will act as a magnet, and the stronger our Positive Thinking, the more Inspiration our magnetic attraction will draw to us.

Therefore, as it relates to our ability to take control of our career, our life, and our destiny, because of the enormous influence that both our positive and negative energy has in our life, I am suggesting that we refer to this as *Magnetic Energy*. By doing so, whenever we speak of the energy necessary to attract Inspiration, it will help for our brains to visualize the actual strength and power of that which we draw to ourselves through this *magnetic energy*.

To further assist our brains to visualize this from a tangible perspective, I would like to spend a minute or so calling to mind the power of magnets.

We have all experienced the power of a magnet. Its size and the amount of its charge determines its pulling power. Picture in your mind as having two horseshoe magnets, one in each hand. We understand each end of the horseshoe is charged with either a positive or negative energy. By holding the two horseshoes end to end, we soon discover that two of the ends will pull toward each other; yet when the ends are reversed the magnet will push away from each other.

Although the magnet is only intended as a visual analogy, however by using it helps us to visualize the fact that we also generate either positive or negative energy, of which will either attract positive Inspiration to us, or will push it away.

Because success and growth are generally considered positive attributes, and failure or stagnation as being negative, then it only follows: Regardless of our endeavor, if our desire is to succeed, then by generating positive magnetic energy through our Positive Thinking we will attract the Inspiration necessary to assure us the success and growth we desire. Not only will we attract the inspiration for the success we seek, but equally as important is that our success will also be drawn toward us, and us toward it through the Inspiration we receive.

Again, picture our magnet. Say I have a pile of metal paper clips and I hold the magnet close to them. The power of the magnet will draw not just one or two, but depending on the magnet's strength, it may draw a dozen or so. And what is just as surprising is that the paper clips will also be attracting others due to the force of energy flowing through them.

Inspiration is attracted to us in the same way. The higher degree of positive thoughts we generate, that is anchored to the foundation of Faith, Trust, and Confidence, the more our Inspiration will provide us the guidance and direction we need to meet our every objective. It's been said that we each have received more than ample inspiration to resolve every issue, and to answer every question we have ever wrestled with. The problem is not with the lack of receiving inspiration;

instead, it's usually with our unwillingness to accept its value and then to act upon it.

Of which once again reverts to the issue of negative thinking or a negative outlook, both of which lack the Faith, Trust, and Confidence that is the needed bedrock of Positive Thinking.

James Allen, who is often a pioneer in the self-help movement of the late 1800s and early 1900s, is often accredited with the statement, *"People do not attract that which they say they want, but rather they attract that which they are."* Let me repeat that. *"People do not attract that which they say they want, but rather they attract that which they are."*

The magnetic energy we generate will attract and ultimately create the experiences that we have in life. *Positive magnetic energy attracts positive outcomes through the positive Inspiration we accept and act upon. Negative magnetic energy, on the other hand, chokes out Inspiration and* attracts a negative result.

That's a critical point for us to understand. The thoughts that will resonate most in our minds will be determined by either the positive or negative magnetic energy that we are generating.

If whatever success we desire is in full alignment with our purpose and who we are, then without a doubt we can be assured that the needed Inspiration will come in both to the degree and within the time necessary to ensure the success we seek to become our best rendition.

The more we align our thoughts and energy to that for which we have a burning desire and are willing to work for, the more detailed our Inspirations will become.

The more we change the consciousness of our primary mindset and the thoughts that resonate most in our mind, the more we can change the result of our life.

Earlier you wrote down the area in which you most desire success. I would invite you to review once again what you have written and then ask yourself, *"As it relates to this success that I desire, do I tend to generate more positive magnetic energy that will attract positive inspiration, or more negative magnetic energy that will push it away? What do I focus on most? Do I focus on all the opportunities available for me to reach my desired success, or do I focus on all the roadblocks or other obstacles standing in my way? Do I focus on all my assets and attributes, my true talents and abilities or do I focus on what I interpret as being my shortcomings and inadequacies?"* When I do generate *Positive Thinking is it grounded in a foundation of Faith, Trust, and Confidence, or does it fall more in line with wishful thinking?*

Ralph Waldo Emerson also validated this very principle when he coined the phrase, *"You become what you think about all day long."*

Regardless of the success or growth that we are working toward (*provided of course that who we are and our purpose in life is in alignment with what we want*), then without a doubt, by generating more positive magnetic energy through Positive Thinking that is grounded in the foundation of faith, trust and confidence, the inspiration needed for the success and growth that we are seeking will always be drawn toward us. When this is our focus, we can be assured that *"We will become what we think about all day long."*

How many times have you observed a successful person and thought to yourself how easy life seems to be for then? It appears that some people have success drop into their laps. It's as if success sought them out. Sometimes it seems that they don't have to work half as hard as the rest of us, yet they seem to achieve twice as much, or more.

When you think about it, isn't that precisely what this basic fact of the principle of cause-and-effect and the generating of positive magnetic energy that will attract the inspiration needed is all about? Successful people have adopted this principle as a way of life, and the success they enjoy is proof of its validity.

Just like our understanding of the law of cause and effect, so too is our understanding of the power we possess to either attract or push away positive Inspiration. It depends entirely on the magnetic energy we are generating and whether its power is positive or negative. Grasping this essential aspect of our foundation is critical to our ability to take control of all aspects of our lives. It's a conscious decision that we have the power to make; we must then determine if we will make that decision or not, as it is totally ours to make.

6

Convictions of Our Beliefs

The general course that our lives take is a mirror of the beliefs and convictions we have about ourselves and the world we live in. By changing those beliefs, we can and will also dramatically change our lives and our destiny.

If you recall, I mentioned that sometimes it is the small things that will produce a dramatic change in the destiny of our life. Although this is true, I think I need to make a clarification. Although changing what we think about ourselves and the world around us will always bring about a dramatic change in our life and destiny, I want to assure you that this may neither be a small task nor an easy objective.

The reality is that what we think about ourselves and the world around us, to a great extent, also involves our self-identity. How we identify ourselves to ourselves and the world is something that we may not be willing or wanting to change. Even if we are wanting and willing to change, it will take a focused effort to do so.

But that does not mean that we cannot make that change. People are doing it every day.

How often do we hear of a young person who once identified herself as being shy and withdrawn go on to become a movie star or a renowned leader in the management of others?

How often have you heard of someone who once identified himself as a slow learner, or even by his own assessment was unable to learn, who then ultimately became the person who invents an item that changed the world, or becomes a giant in an industry?

How often do you hear of a person who once identified herself as being a bit clumsy and awkward, or even to a degree views themselves as being unattractive as an adolescent? Yet this same person goes on to become a high, in-demand model or other type of a celebrity.

So again, changing what we think about ourselves and the world around us may not always be an easy objective or task, but it is possible if the desire is there. This relates to the control that we elect to assume and take over our career and our life, which will without a doubt have a direct impact on our ultimate destiny. It boils down to a decision we must be willing to make before we can become our best.

Critical Convictions

When it comes to the convictions that we hold to be true about ourselves and our world, there are three essential elements of belief that are critical.

Conviction Number 1 is the degree to which we believe in the role that our positive magnetic energy will play toward attracting the inspiration necessary to achieve all the hopes, dreams, and ideas we have for our future.

Whenever we fail to have a firm belief and a strong conviction in the probability that our hopes and dreams are achievable, we will soon discover that our negative magnetic energy will take control of our life. When this happens, we will also find that this negative energy will dramatically block any positive inspirational thoughts that may be otherwise available. Often that which we are blocking will be that very specific inspiration of which is critically needed for us to be the success that we desire and were created to be.

When this happens, our hopes, dreams, and ideas we had for the future all tend to fade into obscurity, and we begin to settle for a life that is both less challenging and for sure substantially less rewarding. Mediocrity, regardless of how you may personally describe that to be, then becomes the standard for which we settle for and become satisfied with.

Conviction Number 2 is the degree of belief that we have in ourselves. When we fail to have a robust unshakable confidence in ourselves and our ability to achieve the success we seek, we tend to develop a defeatist attitude. This attitude can almost always guarantee that we will be willing to settle for much less than we are capable of, as it lacks the basic requirements of Faith, Trust, and Confidence that are the necessary bedrock foundation for Positive Thinking. When this is this case, we can be assured that our negative magnetic energy will take over to attract whatever it may. We can also be assured that a defeatist attitude about ourselves will never attract the quality Inspirations we need to become our best rendition.

Conviction Number 3 goes back to what we discussed earlier when we said that, *"One of the most primary mindsets of people of sustainable success is that they understand and believe that the forces of nature are working in their favor toward their ability to succeed. Therefore, they approach life with an expectation of success."*

Your Magnetic Energy

Whenever people believe that all the cards are stacked against them, chances are the results of their life will become a self-fulfilled prophecy. Remember again the quote from Ralph Waldo Emerson, *"You become what you think about all day long."* When the convictions of our beliefs about the world around us are such that the world will never give us a break, and yes, we even convince ourselves that all the cards are stacked against us, that then becomes what we think about all day long.

At times, the main reason we tend to have that mindset and so often think about it all day long is that to a great extent it will give us the permission, or the excuse for not becoming or achieving all that we have within our ability to become. Let's face it; sometimes when we can blame the world for our state in life, it becomes an easy excuse to take the path of least resistance, so why not take it.

Whenever we develop a negative mindset about either ourselves, the world, or both, it can be almost assured that we will never attract the inspirational thoughts necessary for us to become the best rendition of ourselves that we were meant to be. Even, if by chance, that great inspirational thought does make it past our mental block, chances are, because of our flawed convictions, we will either not recognize the inspiration for what it is, or we will not believe in what it is trying to tell us. Or we will not have enough trust and faith in ourselves to be guided by it.

Again, I ask you to turn to the statement of success that you first identified. Now as you read your statement, ask yourself:

✓ What role do I believe that my general attitude and the magnetic energy that I generate will play in achieving the success I desire?

✓ Do I have an unshakable conviction that the success I desire is entirely achievable?

✓ Do I possess Faith, Trust, and Confidence as the foundational blocks of my Positive Thinking, or is my positive thinking more in tune to mere wishful thinking?

✓ Do I have an unshakable conviction and belief that the world or society or our economic system, or any other force outside of myself is not stacking the cards against me, but rather is in my corner, not only cheering for me, but also depending on me to become the best rendition of myself.

✓ Do I possess a strong expectation of success?

✓ When the gift of inspiration presents itself, can and do I recognize its value and act upon it, or do I permit it to float away like a priceless diamond down the stream?

Now I would also add, if you are not 100% sure regarding any, or all of those questions, I would then say to you, don't change what you wrote, stay committed to your course. There is more for you to learn and we're going to work on getting you there.

Forming the Impression

On two different occasions, I had been invited to deliver the baccalaureate address to high school graduating students. It is always so energizing for me to witness all the impressive hopes and dreams these young people typically have for their future at this point in their lives.

However, so often, a short decade later, it can be heartbreaking to see how so many of them have permitted all those impressive hopes and dreams to be replaced with a life, of which for them, given their inborn talents, would be described as a life of mediocrity or less.

A significant reason behind this change is that they had permitted their negative magnetic energy, and the mental impression they have formed and accepted about themselves, to be their predominant mindset. In other words, they adopted a new identity of themselves, and so once again, *"You become what you think about all day long."*

This mindset and their belief system about themselves and their self-identity evolved to the point of now telling themselves that their hopes and dreams were not realistic for them. Although they may not have a problem with believing that the goals they once held are possible for others, they have convinced themselves that this level of achievement, or the dreams they once held, are not within the scope of reality for them.

After living in the real world and facing a few setbacks and hard knocks, which are merely part of life, they developed a mindset that told them they were foolish to think and believe that they were good enough, or smart enough, or have the right personality, or were born on the right side of the tracks, or whatever rationality they can contrive in their mind that will excuse them from becoming all that they could become. Without a doubt, their negative magnetic energy began to dominate their thoughts and beliefs as to who they were. Their negative energy began to push aside and even block the inspirational thoughts they once treasured. As a result, their dominant negative energy attracted to them all the mediocrity they could handle. Yes, without a doubt, *"They did become what they thought about all day long."*

The primary mindset of our beliefs and the convictions that we hold to be true about ourselves will ultimately dictate our destiny. Our beliefs and convictions will determine the strength of the foundation of the Faith, Trust, and Confidence we have in the thinking of who we are and what we can accomplish toward becoming our best rendition.

Regardless of the task or endeavor, although we may often begin with a high degree of optimism that will generate the Inspiration we need, sad to say, after a few setbacks or tough challenges we often tend to develop a mindset of doubt or skepticism about our ourselves and our chances for success.

We develop a mindset that we are not qualified, or occasionally because the self-identity we have formed we tell ourselves that we don't deserve this. We come up with all sorts of reasons to justify our mindset for not trusting or believing in the value of the Inspirations we are given that sooner or later the conclusion becomes a self-fulfilling prophecy.

The beliefs and convictions we hold about ourselves will always dictate the inspirational thoughts that come our way. In addition, they will determine our willingness to believe in them, act upon them, and to follow them. This also dictates both our immediate results as well as our ultimate destiny.

Franklin D Roosevelt said, *"The only limits of our realization of tomorrow will be our doubts of today,"* [5]

Failure to have an unwavering belief in ourselves, our dreams, and the value of our inspirational thoughts and ideas ultimately translate into doubt and skepticism.

Doubt and skepticism will always stop us dead in our tracks.

Doubt and skepticism will always rob us of a better and more rewarding life.

Doubt and skepticism are what prevents most people from becoming the best rendition of themselves, and sad to say, most of us have not even scratched the surface on becoming the best of ourselves that we have the potential.

Doubt and skepticism are what so often deprive a person of the satisfaction of the gratification and fulfillment in what they do and who they are.

This doubt and skepticism consist of 100% negative magnetic

---

[5] Franklin D. Roosevelt: "Undelivered Address Prepared for Jefferson Day," April 13, 1945.

energy. When we permit this negative magnetic energy to become so strong that it becomes the predominant energy that we consistently generate, it is then when so many give up on believing, trusting, or following those priceless inspirational thoughts that do make it past the barriers that we have set up.

We know that all mammals have brains. We are aware that the brain is merely the physical organ that sends out electrical impulses that tell the rest of our body what to do.

- Our brain tells our heart muscles to pump the blood throughout our bodies.
- Our brain tells our hand to reach up to scratch our nose when it is itching.
- Our brain tells us to pull our hand away from the hot stove.

We know that animals all have almost the same primary physical brain mass as we do, but what they don't have is a mind. Instead, they operate from instinct, and because of that, they have no control over what their brain tells them to do and thus they have absolutely no control over their destiny.

But we humans have more than just a brain. We also possess the intellect of a mind.

- Our mind is what gives us our free will.
- Our mind is what captures and processes the inspirational thoughts that are sent our way.
- Our mind not only gives us the ability to think about what we are thinking about, but it also gives us the ability to change what we are thinking about by simply making the decision to do so.
- Our mind gives us the ability to think freely rather than from instinct alone.

Because of our free-thinking ability, our minds determine who we are, and because of that, our minds determine the mindset from which we operate and thus will determine what we become.

For example, in our neighborhood, several of the neighbors who own dogs have installed a fenceless barrier to keep their beloved pets from leaving the yard. This is done with a very low-voltage electrical wire that is buried around the perimeter of the desired area of confinement. When the dog approaches the boundary line, the wire produces a gentle vibrating electrical shock through a special collar worn by the dog. Although the claim is that this vibrating shock is harmless and painless, after a few times of getting this shock, instinct will tell the dog to stay away from that line in the yard, and for sure do not try to cross it. Because dogs operate from only instinct that permits them the ability to only react, after several months the collar can be removed and the instinct remains, telling the dog not to cross that line.

As the story goes, if a cat were to sit on a hot stove, instinct would tell that cat never to sit on that hot stove again. However, because the cat does not have the power to think with a mind and process its thoughts, instinct will also tell that cat never to sit on that stove, even if it's cold.

Through instinct alone, the dog does not possess the rational understanding of why they get a shock when they approach a certain point in the yard, so they react only to the shock and therefore stay away from it. Likewise, the cat's instinct cannot tell the difference between a stove that's hot or cold, so once burned it will not sit on either. The instinct of an animal can only produce a reaction to a situation.

As humans, because of our intellect, our brains can process the difference between having that collar on or off, or if the stove is hot or cold. So, if the intellect of our minds determines what we think, that means that our brains will believe and thus cause us to act based on whatever our minds tell it that it should think.

Because our minds give us the power to think about what we are thinking about, unlike any other creature, we humans have been given the freedom of will, to produce the thoughts that will provide the information that become the instructions that our brain will accept as being fact, and thus act upon.

Every thought that enters our brain generates a chemical reaction that will in turn generate an electrical impulse, and as stated earlier it is these electrical impulses that generates our magnet energy. Therefore, the thoughts that we tell our brains to think will generate either the positive or the negative magnetic energy that will determine the inspiration we receive, of which in turn will also dictate the journey and destiny of our life.

I grew up with my formative years in the mid to late 1950s to early 1960s. This was the era when smoking cigarettes was the "in thing." It was the era of the good-looking macho Marlboro Man. With a look of pride and power he would stand on the hilltop overlooking his ranch and all the land he controlled. It was when Virginia Slims told the gals that they "came a long way baby," and Salem and Kool cigarettes promoted "a cool refreshing breath of air." Get this, this was the era when several brands of cigarettes had as their advertising slogan that "more doctors recommended their brand than any other."

During this era, smoking for most young lads, and even a lot of young gals, became almost a rite of passage. I began to smoke at around the age of 15. I continued to smoke for approximately the next 40 years. It's not one of my more notable or proud accomplishments, yet that's just the way it was.

During that period, I attempted countless times to quit. To say that

I was addicted is an understatement. I tried everything. I tried quitting cold turkey, I tried the patch, the pill, I even tried the hypnotist, but nothing seemed to work.

One year, while I was getting my annual physical and receiving the same lecture from my physician that I needed to quit smoking as it was terrible for my health. I told my doctor that I was trying and how it was so difficult. Then for the first time, after all the lectures I had received from him, he finally asked me what I was thinking about most while in my efforts to quit. I told him it was obvious; the primary focus on my mind was my desire, or better yet my obsessive cravings I had for a cigarette.

He told me my single biggest problem was that I was focusing on the pain of quitting instead of the positive aspects of being a non-smoker. He said I should focus on all the benefits of not having that constant craving for a cigarette. He suggested I focus on the money I would save and on what other positive and even more enjoyable ways I could use that money. Focus, he said, on how nice it will be to have shirts without burn holes. He suggested that I focus on the fact that my car, my clothes, and even my breath would no longer smell like a dirty old ashtray.

He then gave me the best advice. He said that if I truly wanted to be a former smoker, I needed to tell my brain that is precisely what I am. He told me that my brain would think whatever I tell it, so if I was sincere about wanting to be an ex-smoker, then that's what I needed to believe myself to be. But that would not happen until I first convinced myself of it, and that could not happen until I made a firm decision to focus on convincing my brain that is what it should think, because that is who I am, because that is who I am determined to be.

So, did I quit smoking? Yes. I have now been an ex-smoker for about 15 to 18 years. Was it easy? No; by no means was it easy!

Your Magnetic Energy

Breaking a 40-year habit is never easy. It took some convincing before my brain would accept that I was an ex-smoker, but in the end my mind emerged as the winner.

We all have aspects of our life in which we struggle to improve and specific goals we desire to attain. Our only chance to emerge as a winner is when we begin to refocus our mind and brain from the negative to the positive. As free-thinking humans, we can think about what we are thinking about, therefore we can also change what our brain is thinking about.

Remember this: Our mind has the ability, the right, and the authority to tell our brain whatever it is we want it to both think and believe. Although at times it may take some work to successfully convince our brains to change the thoughts it is thinking, still at the end of the day, if our combined faith, trust, and confidence is strong enough, and if the belief we have in our mind is solid enough, then our mind will emerge as the winner.

The crucial point is, if our Faith, Trust, and Confidence are strong enough and the belief we have in our mind is solid enough. That is the key. Before our mind can emerge as the real winner, it will take more than a mere suggestion or even a wishful thought. It takes the desire and the believability we have in ourselves to successfully tackle any issue we hope to overcome, or goal we wish to achieve, thus, to become our best rendition. That means it must be more than a few wishful thoughts or words we are trying to put into our brains.

As was stated earlier, every thought that enters our brain generates a chemical reaction which also causes an electrical impulse. When this chemical reaction and the electrical impulse are combined, it creates an emotion or a feeling. The more focused our thought, the stronger our feelings become. Ultimately it will be the strength of the emotion or feeling that is generated from both our heart and mind that will determine the message our brain will accept. The strength of our emotion will be the impression that is implanted in and accepted by our brain.

Because this is so important, to help solidify my point I'd like to give several examples of everyday emotions we often deal with.

It's not unusual that we extend the words of "thank-you" or "thanks" countless times throughout the day. The waitress refills our coffee cup, and we say thanks. Someone holds the door for us, and we say thank you. In such cases, our gratitude is a matter of courtesy that we extend to someone who does something for us. It's a matter of a simple, polite behavior or gesture of which we give little thought to and generally with very little, if any, emotional feeling that's impressed upon us.

Now compare that to the heartfelt gratitude you are likely to have when that certain someone in your life does something for you that you viewed as very special. Most likely, you experienced a sincere emotional reaction. You experienced a genuine feeling that not only went from your mind to your brain, but it was also an emotion that extended from your heart. It was only then that your brain believed that your gratitude was honest and genuine. So, once again, it's the strength of our heartfelt emotions that will determine if our brain will accept that which our mind is telling it.

Another quick example: Say I have a rare opportunity to be a passenger in the rear seat of an Air Force Blue Angel Jet. Assuming this is my first experience in such an airplane, and the pilot is preforming the acrobatic twist and turns they are well-known for. Regardless of how many times my mind tries to tell my brain that I am fearless and have no anxiety, the chances are my brain won't accept this thought as being valid. Why? Because I will be sending mixed messages. My emotions of fear and anxiety will smother out the sound of anything my mind may be trying to convince my brain of.

One more example: Statistics indicate that one of the greatest apprehensions we have as an adult is that of speaking in public. Why is that? Most three-year-olds have no problem or concern with speaking out in a group. However, give that child another 20 years or so, and chances are just the thought of it will petrify them. Some even to the extent that it can make them physically ill. No, it's not a fear we are born with; instead, it's a belief that our mind has adopted and convinced our brain of due to some past emotional experience. The chances are that somewhere along the line there was a negative experience that impacted them emotionally. It was this negative emotional experience that their brain had accepted and convinced them that it is in their best interest to avoid public speaking.

When our mind delivers the proper messages to our brain, it causes our entire being, consisting of our heart, our mind, and our brain to all work together. This results in the rest of our body following through to make up the total package of the persona we project. It is this persona that will produce the person that both we and others will see us to be.

You see, our brain alone cannot tell the difference between fiction and reality. That is left up to our human mind and heart to ascertain. The certainty of our faith, the depth of our trust, and strength of our confidence will ultimately determine the emotional message that is accepted by our brains as being reality.

The more our heart, mind, brain, and body, work together toward generating positive magnetic energy, the more positive effect we will notice in our everyday life. We will soon discover that even the pace, stride, and cadence of our walk will display the positive magnetic energy that we are now generating.

We will discover that our eyes will transmit a look of optimism and self-confidence, rather than that of a pessimistic "poor me" victim, or someone who is steeped in worry, anger or other negative emotions.

We will also begin to realize the thoughts we both have and project toward others will be more positive than negative. Our conversations will become more optimistic and upbeat. We will project an aura of creativity vs. stagnation or entitlement.

Once our heart, mind, brain, and body begin working together toward changing the magnetic energy we generate, we will discover that the transformation of our outward appearance, as well as their inward attitude we have toward both ourselves and others will soon become habitual. As with any habit, the more it becomes what we do, the more our brains will recognize and believe that it is who we are, of which will then evolve into our very nature.

When our mind can emotionally experience the benefits of attaining any goal we have a burning desire for, and can further accept the belief that we are the person who we want to be, we will discover that not only will we generate positive inspiration, but just as important, when those positive inspirations do come our way, we will not only recognize them for the priceless diamonds they are, but our faith, trust, and confidence will enable to us to act upon them. I once again remind you of the words of wisdom from Ralph Waldo Emerson when he said, "You become what you think about all day long."

A bit earlier, I talked about my struggles, and my many failed attempts to quit smoking. Only after my mind could become emotionally attached to all the benefits of being a non-smoker and I had a clear vision of me being a non-smoker, was I also able to become the master of my destiny.

I now invite you make this personal to yourself. Review what you wrote earlier concerning the areas of success you desire most. Regardless of what your goal may be, until your heart and mind can become emotionally involved in the benefits of attaining the destiny of that goal, your brain will never be convinced that you can attain it.

Bottom line, you may desire success and may think success, but if you feel a failure, you will never attract the success you are capable of or deserving. Why? Because you are sending a mixed message, and our brains will not accept such a message.

Without a doubt, when our heart, mind, brain, and body are all working together to create positive magnetic energy that one can emotionally feel and believe, only then will we find ourselves traveling down a new path in life. A path that will lead us on our journey to becoming our best rendition.

Early in my business career I read the book *Think and Grow Rich* by Napoleon Hill, which was first published in 1937. In it he made a statement that has stuck with me all these years. It's a statement that I not only have never forgotten but also one that I have accepted as absolute truth and have shared countless times with others. That statement is: *"Whatever the mind of man can conceive and believe, he can achieve."* [6]

Because of our ability to be free thinkers and to think about what we are thinking about, we also have the power to change the emotional feeling and image that we want our mind to plant into our brain. As a result we likewise have the power to generate either the positive or the negative magnetic energy that will produce either the positive or negative thinking that will determine the inspirational thoughts that are attracted to us, and equally as important, the inspirational thoughts that we are willing to accept and follow.

James Allen, of who as I mentioned earlier is believed to be the father of the self-help movement during the late 1800 and early 1900's once said, *"Belief is the basis of all action, and this being so, the belief*

[6] *Think and Grow Rich* by Napoleon Hill; Sound Wisdom First Addition 1937

that dominates the heart or mind is shown in the life we have." [7]

Successful people have learned how to apply their positive magnetic energy so to attract not only this positive image about themselves, but also to manage their everyday actions in a manner that will push away the negative thinking that is created through doubt, skepticism, fear, or a defeatist and negative impression we hold to be true of ourselves and the outlook we have on life.

Look online at any bookselling website for books about positive thinking, or positive mental attitude, or believing in oneself. You will find several thousands of books on these combined topics. This abundance should provide an indication of the reality that the *"how"* we process our thoughts and what we tell our brain to think is so critical to the inspirational thoughts that are so critical for us to attract the success we desire and the journey we wish to take, regardless of how we may describe that success or journey to be.

The great Michelangelo once said that most people are frustrated not because they aim too high and miss but rather because they aim too low and hit it.

It was Zig Ziglar who always told the story about the flea trainers.

According to his story, fleas can jump as high as 150 times their own height. To put that in perspective; If you are 5 feet 6 inches tall, that would mean that you could jump over 800 feet in the air. But fleas can also be trained to believe that they can only jump to a height that is much less than their inborn ability.

To do this, fleas are placed into a glass jar. Then the lid is put on the jar. At first, the fleas will jump high enough so that they will consistently hit themselves against the lid of the jar. After they have been hitting the lid so many times, they train themselves to jump to a height that is just short of the lid.

---

[7] *As We Think, So We Are* by James Allen

After they have been doing this for a while, the lid of the jar can be removed, and surprisingly, the fleas continue to jump at the same safe height as if the lid were still on.[8]

Bottom line, through instinct, they had trained themselves to accept the limit they imposed upon themselves, and they conditioned themselves to remain in the safe zone of not hitting themselves against the lid of the jar. But what had become absolutely devastating for them, is that they had also conditioned themselves to remain trapped in the jar forever.

Everyone has heard of the actor Sylvester Stallone. He has played in numerous action movies but is probably most noted for staring in the *Rocky* series of films that are still being rerun today.

However, what most do not know about him is the difficult journey he traveled before he hit it big. His story is a real example of someone's determination not to remain trapped in that flee jar but kept pushing forward so he could jump as high as he did.

Stallone came to New York with a dream of becoming an actor. It was a dream that he had an emotional attachment. Without any doubt it was due to the strength of the foundation of his Faith, Trust, and Confidence that provided the positive energy to pursue his dream. But like many aspiring actors, he was also flat broke. But through sheer determination and a strong belief in himself, he pursued by knocking on every door he could. Time after time he was told he did not have what it takes to make it in Hollywood. But against all the odds he persisted.

When he reached what many would describe as being the lowest point in his life, he was gifted with an inspiration that proved to be life changing. Due to the degree of faith, trust, and confidence he possessed, along with his passionate belief in himself, he acted upon

---

[8] *The Worst Peanut in Town* by Zig Ziglar; Tyndale House Publishers 1988

his inspiration and wrote the script for *Rocky*.

Once completed he began promoting his work to movie producers and directors. To his credit it was well received. It's reported that He was offered, which for him, being a flat broke actor at the time, was a substantial amount of $350,000. But it came with a heartbreaking stipulation. You see, the inspiration he received was twofold, the first part was to write the script, but the second part was that he would star in the movie. But the caveat for the sale of the script was that he would not be the star in the film.

But he persisted. His mind had convinced his brain that he would succeed. There was no mixed message. Because he refused to become his own flee trainer, he finally succeeded. We all know the rest is history. Stallone went on to not only star in his first scripted movie, but it went on to be made into a series of seven additional movies, all of which were box office hits. All of which he stared as the lead actor.

Sylvester Stallone persisted by having his mind convince his brain that he was "the" actor that could deliver what was needed to make the movie a hit. He refused to permit negative energy to influence the positive thinking required to generate the inspiration that provided the journey he followed and the success he enjoyed. He was passionate about his convictions to the degree that no one could convince him of taking any other route other than the one he knew would permit him to become the best rendition of himself.

The chances are that most of us at one time or another have been guilty of being our own flea trainer. We have permitted our mind to tell our brain what limits we should either impose or expect for ourselves. When we do so, we also place boundaries on our inspirational thoughts.

We have permitted our mind to tell our brain to focus on the negative of why we *can't* accomplish a given task, rather than on the positive of how and why we can make the journey necessary to achieve the success we seek. We have permitted our mind to tell our brains that we should settle for less than becoming the best rendition of ourselves because that is all that we are entitled to, or worthy of, or capable of accomplishing. We have placed a self-imposed lid on our inspired thoughts.

But we are worthy and capable of more than pure mediocrity. We have both a right and a responsibility to ask for life to pay what we know we are worth. If we must be a flea trainer, then we must be determined to train our fleas that there is no lid and that we can jump as high as we can, and if that is 800 feet, then so be it. We will make a vow to ourselves that we will never again become frustrated because we have set the bar too low and hit it. Instead, we will strive for the satisfaction and fulfillment that we set it high and reached it.

I challenge you now to once again turn to the one area of success you wrote down earlier. Be honest with yourself and list several possible areas when you have become your own flea trainer. List several ways in which you are permitting your mind to plant into your brain some of the doubts and skepticism you may have as it relates to the journey necessary to achieve the success you desire. I challenge you to honestly discern if you are aiming high enough or are you merely taking the path of the least resistance. Do you desire that goal to the degree that you can become emotionally "fired up" when you consider the benefits you will receive "when" you attain that goal? If so do you now think it's time to rewrite your goal so that it will more accurately describe the journey you need to take to lead to the success that you are both capable of and have the emotional conviction that you will achieve.

7

Paradigm of Our World

Reality is such that we humans typically operate from the premise that when specific ideas, beliefs, and even theories become the norm of acceptance, they become the paradigm or model from which we operate.

The paradigm from which we operate our life is a collection of all the values, practices, and experiences of our past that we have ingrained into our brain, and most often even our subconscious mind, to the degree that we accept them as "that's just the way things are."

Whenever we adopt a belief to the extent that it becomes a part of our paradigm, that belief or experience either consciously or subconsciously becomes an integral part of our belief system and the standard from which we live our life. It is that belief system, or that paradigm if you will, that can ultimately dictate the journey we take that will shape our destiny.

As an example: When I had the real estate brokerage company, while there was always that exception, for the most part I could usually predict reasonably close as to what a new agent would earn during his or her first year in the business. As a rule, their earnings for their first year in business would be in the general area of what they had been earning in the past. Why? Because their paradigm was formed based on the belief they adopted as to the level of income they should expect "for themselves." For example, an agent who had been accustomed to earning in the area of $30,000 to $40,000 a year, that is about the general limits of income they would earn during that first year. On the other hand, a new agent who had earned between $50,000 and $60,000 in their previous profession or job would likely earn that much or more because that was what they expected from themselves. It was what their mind had convinced their brain that they were capable of. It was their belief system that provided the expectation of the paradigm that shaped their destiny.

On the other hand, for a new agent who had earned between $30,000 and $40,000 in their previous profession or job, the thought of earning $50,000 to $60,000 went beyond their belief system. It was outside of their paradigm. It went beyond what the mind could convince their brain of. For a new agent who had previously earned less than $40,000, it was almost impossible to get emotionally engaged and fired up at the thought of earning over $60,000. Although that new agent may have wanted to earn $60,000-plus, and maybe even considered it possible, until that agent could emotionally feel it as being a reality, the likelihood of earning at their true potential was greatly diminished.

Before this new agent can earn what he or she is truly capable of, and yes, even entitled to, this earning amount must first become part of their belief system and the paradigm of their world. Recall again;

our beliefs are based on the foundational blocks of Faith, Trust, and Confidence that support the Positive Thinking that will provide the emotional convictions necessary to generate the inspiration we need to produce what we are indeed capable of. Without that foundation, our thinking is reduced to only wishful thinking. Regardless of how much that new agent would wish for that level of income, until it became part of the paradigm of their life and belief, it would remain no more than mere wishful thinking.

Negative magnetic energy will attract and form a belief system that will create the paradigm that will become the roadblock or the lid on the flea jar that prevents us from advancement and forever entrapping us in our present state.

On the other hand, positive magnetic energy will attract the paradigm to form a belief system that gives us the permission and the confidence to push forward and move beyond our current state of life.

You would be among the rare and unusual person if you don't have some baggage from the past that can become the excuse, or at least the tendency to hold you back from accomplishing all that you can become, thus becoming the best rendition of yourself possible.

Quite some years ago I had a close friend who by all outward appearances was living what most would describe as almost a fairy tale life. Both he and his wife had good jobs with promising careers. They had two children, both boys, four and six years old at the time. Both were as cute as a button and as healthy as could be. All appeared to be good. Suddenly the world changed for this all-American family.

One evening after the two boys were bathed and tucked into bed, my friend's wife informed him that they needed to talk. During the two hours that followed he was informed that she was in love with someone else, that she never intended to hurt him, but it just happened, and that's just the way things were. She said she had filed for divorce and he would be officially served with the papers on the following day.

He said this came as a total surprise and shock. His claim at the time was that he had no warning and did not see any signs to indicate there was a problem in their marriage. Regardless if there was or not, what ensued was a hard-fought, very bitter divorce battle. They fought about every paper clip, rubber band, and plastic cup they had. The two boys became the pawns for the tool of revenge.

Once the divorce was finalized, they both emerged as bitter losers. Although they were awarded joint custody of the children, they continued to battle over every detail. My friend evolved into an angry and bitter individual who was very vocal of his distrust of women. He swore he would never subject himself to another.

This destructive attitude lasted for at least five years before he finally began to turn his life around. This turn around did not occur until he made the conscious decision to do so. Although many of the events of his life were outside of his control, and yes, from his perspective he was dealt a lousy hand, the paradigm of the beliefs that he elected to form as to the way the world was for him and his two boys was totally within his control.

The reality is, we are who and what we are today because that is what we have chosen to be. We need to take the responsibility to use what we have been empowered with to become the best rendition of ourselves as possible. We only need to give ourselves permission to do so, and then convince our brains to kick into action to get the job done.

It's our responsibility, as intelligent adults with a free will, to change the magnetic energy we are generating from that of the negative to the positive. To do this, it may require a heart-to-heart talk with ourselves. You may need a full discernment process regarding the paradigm that you operate from and the thoughts and ideas that provide the perception you have of your life and world.

Therefore, you should ask yourself, "Is the current paradigm of my belief system of who I am and the world I live in holding me back and keeping me entrapped in whatever jar I may find myself in, or does it encourage me to move forward, to jump as high as I can, and become all that I can become?"

Alcoholics Anonymous promotes the basic tenet that one cannot fix a problem until it is first acknowledged. We need to be honest with ourselves, to recognize and name whatever our paradigm may be that is holding us back and preventing us from making the journey necessary to achieve the success that we both desire and is within our ability to achieve.

Stephen Covey said, *"Until a person can deeply and honestly say, I am what I am today because of the choices I made yesterday, that person cannot say, I choose otherwise."*[9]

Our positive magnetic energy is hard at work when the convictions of the beliefs we have about ourselves and our world are focused on the positive opportunities that life has to offer. This positive energy gives us the full understanding that we, and we alone, have the power to change and create our belief system.

Whatever the convictions of the beliefs you have about yourself and the world around you, it is those beliefs that will determine if your positive magnetic energy attracts an attitude of "I know I can" or if your negative magnetic energy attracts an attitude of "I'll try, but I doubt if I can." Or worse yet, "why try, I already know that I can't."

The convictions of our beliefs will determine our ability to recognize, believe, and act upon the Inspired thoughts that come our

---

[9] *Daily Reflections for Highly Effective People* by Stephen R. Covey; Touchstone 1994

way. The choice is entirely ours to make. We have a choice about what our mind tells our brain to think. We have a choice as to the paradigm of the world we choose to be a reality for us. Once we can accept the fact that these are choices for us to make, then the next step is for us to take the control necessary to implement the decisions for the opportunities that are in our best interest.

8

Be True to Yourself

One of the many quotes that William Shakespeare is known for is, "This above all: to thine own self be true, and it must follow, as the night the day, thou canst not then be false to any man."

The discussion in this chapter is, by intention and design, positioned in about in the center of the book. By doing so, the points that are made help to round out and solidify the foundation that we have been working on thus far in the book. But equally as important, it will help us to better utilize the tools that wil be discussed in future chapters.

If you recall from Chapter One, we discussed the definition of success. In it, the second sentence states that success is, "A growth and improvement that is the result of us using to the very best of our capability all the talents and abilities we have been entrusted with to become our best rendition." That statement could not be truer. However, before any of us can fully use to the best of our capability all our talents and abilities to become our best rendition, it is necessary that we first accomplish what's in the first sentence of our definition, which states, "Success is a sustaining pattern of growth and improvement in one's life that leads to becoming our true self."

For anyone to find their true self can be as valuable as uncovering the Hope Diamond. I can't help but wonder how many doctors, lawyers, plumbers, farmers, and businesspeople who are struggling every day, doing what they do only because of an obligation they felt to either follow in someone else's footsteps or to live up to someone's expectations.

Anytime we are not doing or becoming in life what we were meant to be; we cannot grow into our best rendition, thereby fulfilling the purpose for which we were created. Unfortunately, the world is filled with good people who are in every occupation and profession, but who are not being true to themselves. These are good people who are operating at only an average level compared to what they can become for both themselves, their families, and their communities.

But being true to ourselves encompasses more than merely our job or profession. It also embodies the "how" and the "why" we do what we do, and that necessitates that we first have a better grasp on knowing and understanding who we are.

To have an explicit knowledge and understanding of who we are is a critical ingredient in the foundation we build. It could be said that when we fail to honestly know ourselves and do not have a clear understanding of who we are, it is then that we are typically unaware of both the form and function of our life.

Think about it, everything that we discussed in all the previous chapters would have little meaning, much less value, without first having actual knowledge and understanding of ourselves.

Throughout this book, we discuss the importance of the journey we take to become our best rendition, which mandates that we are true to ourselves. It is then and only then that our life's journey will provide the quality of the fulfillment and satisfaction for which we strive. Staying true to yourself is a matter of personal integrity and self-respect. Being true to yourself can lead to independence, confidence, happiness, and the ability to navigate through life more effectively, leading to that sense of self-fulfillment and satisfaction that you've given your best self to the world.

So, in this chapter we will discuss a few key points regarding accomplishing that critical task. We begin our discussion on how we first get to know and understand ourselves better, why it's important, and how we can better live our lives being true to that person who we know we are, or at least think we are.

While it is true that most of us feel that we have a high degree of certainty that we do know and understand the person that we are, however, psychological studies indicate otherwise. One such study indicates that people who said they had a clear sense of themselves were better at predicting what they would do in the future. [10] In other words, the clarity of that crystal ball of predicting our future is tied to the clarity we have of ourselves.

As we had discussed earlier in Chapter Seven, the paradigm that we have established for our life also plays into our self-identity. Unfortunately, at times our paradigm may be hardwired with built-in self-deception. This of course, makes the clarity of the path much foggier. To get yourself over any hurdle you first need to acknowledge that this self-deception exists to the degree that it does. Often when

[10] Gary W. Lewandowski Jr. & Natalie Nardone (2012) Self-concept Clarity's Role in Self–Other Agreement and the Accuracy of Behavioral Prediction, Self and Identity, 11:1, 71-89, DOI: 10.1080/1529868.2010.512133

it is not acknowledged it can cause a misdirection in the path we should be following. For sure it will not only confuse what our mind is trying to tell our brain, but it will also make it almost impossible to get emotionally fired up, as down deep our entire being, consisting of our brain, our mind, our heart and soul knows all too well that we are not being honest with our self.

But before we go any further down that path, it's essential that we first have a clear understanding up front of what being true to yourself does not entail.

Being true to yourself does not mean that one adopts a selfish attitude that would imply that life is all about me; therefore, the world should, or even must, adapt to my way of thinking. As a simple example. If you view receiving an uninvited hug from the opposite sex's as offensive, and I see it as respectful, which one of us is permitted to be ourselves?

Although being true to ourselves is important, as intelligence adults we also need to rethink what we mean by it. In the real world, we all adapt and filter our decisions based on the audience. How I relate to my adult children will be different from how I react with my work colleagues. And I relate to each family member and my colleagues differently based upon a realistic consideration of their preferences and values. So, we must transcend a rigid notion of authenticity and instead figure out what it means to be true to ourselves, our values and principles, while not asking others to compromise their values, thoughts and principles that are important to them.

Another important point: being true to ourselves does not permit us to take the easy way out by saying "that's who I am, therefore, that's who I will always be." I may be the same person I was twenty years ago; however, hopefully my life experiences have permitted me to grow and mature. I like to think that where I am at today gives me the advantage of wisdom that I did not have in my 20s.

A culturally intelligent approach to life and work provides us with the opportunity to respect the perspectives, values, and norms of others without leaving our own principles and values entirely behind. As we broaden our scope by seeing through the eyes of others, we rarely abandon everything we thought and did before, but we may evolve to take on other perspectives and values that fit as well.

Therefore, if being true to myself is not only about me or who I am, then what does it entail? To best answer that we need to look at it as a three-part equation.

The first is getting to know ourselves as the person we are. After all, how can we begin to remain true to something that we do not have full knowledge? Getting to know ourselves is not always an easy task, in fact, sometimes it can be a downright daunting endeavor, but it's a journey that we must be willing to take if we are serious about becoming our best rendition.

The second part of our equation is gaining an understanding of our self. It's one thing to genuinely know ourselves, and it's something altogether different to understand what makes us tick, and why we do what we do when we do it.

In our First Chapter, we discussed the difference between what we do or how we do it, and how that is different compared to the "why" we do it. Merely getting to know ourselves can be compared to *what* we do or *how* we do it whereas the understanding of ourselves could be more like the *why* we do it.

It is only when we first have a knowledge of ourselves, and then an understanding of the "why" of ourselves that the third part of the equation comes into play. This consists putting together the What, How, and Why, and then being true to ourselves as the person we now know and understand ourselves to be. To put it another way, once we have the knowledge and understanding of who we are, it's vital that we don't compromise the true nature of who we are, but instead remain true to ourselves, and don't wear the false mask of pretending we are someone who we are not.

Knowing Your True Self

There are volumes of books written on the topic of getting to know yourself. Additionally, some folks spend thousands upon thousands of dollars with their psychiatrist, in one session after another, to get to the bottom of this very topic of getting to know their true self. For some this can be a lifelong endeavor that can be an ever-evolving process, yet, setting aside any psychological issues, I offer the following ten simple areas of self-examination. Consider this as a layman's suggestions for a starting point of getting to know ourselves a bit better.

Get to know your personality

Understanding your personality is maybe the first key. In one respect you have the collective opinion of others, but you also have your database of information that comprise of your everyday actions and attitudes that can be the real interpretation of what your personality is like, and who you are in your private moments, and how that compares to the persona you display in public.

The idea is to get to know your personality inside and out. It's essential that you get to know firsthand not only what and who you are, but also what and who you are not. Try to comprehend and understand what makes you react a certain way in life's countless situations. Ask yourself "Why did I do that?" then be honest with your answer.

Who are you behind your name? What are your characteristic traits? What are your personality traits that shine when you're among friends? What traits shine when you're with strangers? What is the facade you most often portray to the outside world?

What is your demeanor when you have a good day and everything is going your way, as well as on those bad days when it appears that the entire universe is unwilling to cooperate with you and your plans? How do you react to the world around you, especially when you are under pressure? Can you maintain a level head, or do you tend towards becoming flustered, frustrated and short tempered?

Getting an honest grip on your personality is an essential aspect of getting to know your true self.

Get to know your core values and principles

Your core values consist of the moral codes you have adopted, of which often can include the religious and spiritual principles you hold near and dear to your heart. Having said that however, as often the case may be, what we may claim or even try to convince ourselves as to what our core values and spiritual beliefs are, may not always be the bedrock we stand on or that our actions and attitudes reflect. To honestly get to know our self, it's important that we make a list of our top five or six most sacred core principles, and list them in order of their importance. These are the five or six that we would go to all lengths to remain committed to and are unwilling to compromise.

Regardless if it relates to your work, your home, your spirituality, or in any other aspects of your life, consider which of your values and principles would be unnegotiable? Is it honesty and integrity, or are you more prone to success or maybe security? It doesn't always have to be an either-or situation. Instead, maybe it's a matter of how far the scales must tip in one direction or another that may tell us more of who we are. Is it a dedication to do the job right and right the first time, or do you tend to tip the scales more toward getting the objective off your plate, regardless of what it takes? Do you value loyalty above personal agenda; responsibility above ambition, or innovation above the status quo? Do you value relationships over monetary success? If you are honest with your self-assessment you may be surprised as to how your real core values may be a bit different compared to what you often try to project.

Having an explicit knowledge of the core values and principles that define who we are is a critical milestone that will help to identify our true selves to our self.

Get to know your aspirations

What kind of aspirations do you have for your career, your life and your destiny?

When what we aspire to is authentically routed in the foundation of the Faith, Trust, and Confidence that is generated by our Positive Thinking, we can be assured that together they will reflect your most deep seated hopes and dreams of which will lead you down the pathway to our future.

Start getting to know the details of what you aspire to for your life. Once you have that locked in, don't be willing to settle for anything less. Become emotionally attached to both the journey and the destiny that your aspirations and inspirations are leading you. Embrace the details and specifics of each one of them.

For example, if you aspire to be a musician, ask yourself: What instrument do you want to play? What level of proficiency do you want to attain? How big of a part of your life would it be? And on and on until you know everything about your dream.

Be proud of and committed to your aspirations. Don't hide or consider them to be only a "pipe dream." Listen carefully and take seriously the inspirations you may be receiving regarding the details of the path available for you to follow and achieve that what you are aspiring to.

In an article posted on April 20, 2016, in *Psychology Today*, Author Gregg Levoy commented, "Dreams tell you what you know about something, what you really feel. They point you toward what you need for growth, integration, expression, and the <u>health</u> of your relationships to person, place, and thing. They can help you fine-tune your direction and show you your unfinished business. They're meaning machines. And they never lie. Author Tom Robbins once said that dreams don't come true; they are true. When we talk about our dreams coming true, we're talking about our ambitions." [11]

It's important to have a clear understanding of your aspirations, hopes, and dreams for they are also telling you what you are capable of achieving so to become your best rendition. They are both the seeds and the offspring of the inspiration that's generated by our positive thinking. Having a clear understanding of our hopes, dreams and aspirations are an integral part of getting to know your true self.

Get to know your likes and dislikes

What are your likes, and just as important, what are your dislikes? A pure and innocent question but knowing this about yourself gives you confidence into who you are. A lot of people go through life liking what's popular and disliking what's not "cool." That can be like trying to hit a moving target as it moves with the latest fad of society.

It's vital that we not only take the time to define our likes and dislikes, but it's also essential that we evaluate those likes and dislikes to the degree that we can conclude as to why those likes and dislikes are important to us. What is it about our personality, our core values,

---

[11] https://www.psychologytoday.com/us/blog/passion/201604/dreams-dont-come-true-they-are-true

our upbringing, and our past that attribute to the "why" of those likes and dislikes?

Defining your likes and especially your dislikes requires a level of discernment and intuitiveness, especially when weighing against the latest politically correctness of society to that of who we know ourselves to be. But that is where a degree of wisdom comes in. Spending three hours with an extended family member may not coincide with your preference, but maybe it does coincide with a higher personal choice that may lend itself to your core value of respect and kindness toward others.

Defining and understanding your likes and dislikes will go a long way in knowing yourself.

How would you like others to perceive you?

We naturally would like everyone to perceive us as being a good, honest, hardworking, and reputable person. However, going beyond that, if we want to know our true self, we need to pose the further questions of Who is the person that we would like for our spouse to perceive us to be? Who is the person that we wish for our children to see us as being? Who do we want for our employer, our employees, our coworkers to perceive us to be? In each or any of the above, is that the same person that we would want our pastor to perceive us to be.

Often, we tend to wear a mask to conceal our true self, especially when it comes to the impression that we would like to leave with others as to the person who we are. There are times when we wear that mask simply because we do not feel that we can live up to their expectations, while at other times we may not feel comfortable in exposing that true self of who we know (or think we know) ourselves to be. Coming to grips with the reality of how we would like others to perceive us, and how close that comes to the person who we really are is an essential step in gaining our actual knowledge of who we are.

What Is your most fundamental self-limiting belief about yourself?

It's only natural that we all have a place in the sand where we would draw the line and say that this is as far as I can go. We all have both physical and mental limits of where we draw that line. In our quest to become our best rendition it is essential that we understand those limits, not only for a better knowledge of who we are, but equally as important is to know where our most significant growth potential may exist. Having an actual understanding of our self-limiting beliefs about ourselves will also help us to realize the degree of which we have become our own flee trainer.

Define your hats and roles

Most of us have various hats that we wear that consist of roles that are important to us. Understanding ourselves also includes our need to comprehend the various roles that we have in life. These may consist of your marital or parental status. Maybe it consists of the multiple hats or functions you play in your professional life, your social life with your friends and extended family, as well as your service to your church and community.

The more rolls of responsibility that we have in life, the more temptations we may face to negotiate our desire and ability to remain true to ourselves. This can happen when our lines of priority become compromised. Although it's impossible not to cross those lines at times, for us to be true to ourselves it's important that we make every attempt to reduce those situations as often as possible.

For example, attending a recital or a sporting event for one of my children is naturally a higher priority than meeting with a client. However, reality can sometimes set in, in as much as I also understand my responsibility to provide for the financial wellbeing of my family. In which case maybe meeting with a client is necessary and in the best interest of not only myself and my career, but that of my family as well. The key is whether we are following our need to meet our responsibilities or are we using it as an excuse. Are we letting our professional ambitions needlessly take priority over personal relationships? It is for this reason why it's essential that we not only understand the various roles that we play in life but also rank those roles in order of importance and their priority to us. If we are honest to ourselves as to the ranking we assign, it may be an awakening as to knowing ourselves better. Once again, it is impossible for us to be true to ourselves if we do not have a full understanding of our self.

Define your insecurities and your inadequacies

Notice that the title of this sub-section did not ask if you had any insecurities or feeling of inadequacies. Instead, the assumption is that it is a given that you do—we all do—to one degree or another.

Your insecurities may include relationships, your financial wellbeing or even your ability to stand up to the expectation of others. They may stem from how you view your body; do you look upon yourself as being too tall, too short, too thin or overweight?

How about your inadequacies? What if any mental or physical inadequacies do you wrestle with? Are you a bad speller or a slow reader? Do you find math exceptionally difficult? Do you lack even basic mechanical inclinations?

The reality is that we all suffer from some degree of either insecurities or inadequacies or both. As a rule, our insecurities are self-perceived based on past experiences. A broken relationship, financial hardships, or even getting teased on the playground, any of which may lead to our feelings of insecurities. Being embarrassed over a poor grade in school or having continued difficulties in accomplishing a specific task that you find others doing quite easily may attribute to your feelings of both insecurities and inadequacies.

To uncover the "who" we are and the "why" we act the way we do is critical. It's important that we understand the total story that brought us to where we are at today. Our willingness to explore our past is important in our journey to understanding ourselves and becoming who we aspire to be. Research has shown that it isn't just the things that happened to us that define who we become, but how much we were able to make sense of what's happened to us.

Understanding the unresolved major and minor traumas from our history can help to inform us of the ways in which we act and react today. Studies have even shown that life story coherence has a "statistically significant relationship to our psychological well-being." [12]

The fact that we have whatever insecurities or inadequacies we may perceive is not the issue; our unwillingness to first recognize and then to take ownership of them is where the problem arises. Until we do so, we will never get a proper grip on knowing our self, much less conquering the demons that we may often wrestle with.

What do you believe is the meaning of your life?

Wow, this is a big one, but it is one that must be tackled if we have a desire to know our self. In Chapter Two we discussed that each of us was created for a purpose, and the necessity to uncover that purpose. In this question, you are asked to evaluate how your purpose defines the meaning of your life. To put it another way, how would you describe what it is that brings meaning to your life and does that meaning define the purpose of your life.

---

[12] Baerger, Dana Royce and Dan P. McAdams. 1999. "Life Story Coherence and its Relation to Psychological Well-Being". Narrative Inquiry 9:1, 69–96 Published on line 01 January 1999 https://doi.org/10.1075/ni.9.1.05bae

If I am a person who believes that my purpose in life is to climb as high on the corporate ladder as I can. Then what brings meaning to my life may be different than if I believe my real purpose is to make a positive mark on this world as a result of the type of spouse, parent, and overall person I am.

Irrespective of my role in life, how I wrap who I am, and what I do, into the core values I hold to be true for me will help me to both understand and define how my life has meaning and what I view as my purpose.

As a general statement, how one may find meaning in life can be better described by who I am, more so than what I do. So, if that's the case, I again ask, "What do you believe is the meaning and purpose of your life."

Until one can have even a rudimentary knowledge of how to identify the meaning of life, it is almost impossible to understand our purpose, thus having a complete understanding of oneself.

Assignment

Before we can even hope to become our best rendition, it is critical that we first have knowledge of who we are as a person. Because this is such a significant undertaking, it requires more than merely reading the words in a book. Therefore, I am going to do something that most authors would never do. I'm inviting you to put the book down for at least 24 hours, or more if needed. During that period, I challenge you to pray about, meditate or deliberate (whichever best fits your personality) on the ten questions that were asked in this section of the book.

St. Augustine is attributed to saying, *"Men go abroad to wonder at the heights of mountains, at the huge waves of the sea, at the long courses of the rivers, at the vast compass of the ocean, at the circular motions of the stars, and they pass by themselves without wondering."* [13]

I encourage you, do not pass by yourself without wondering. You may be surprised. The chances are that you will discover that there is a lot more to you, and about you than you would imagine. The chances are that you will find that you are only scratching the surface as to what you can offer to yourself, your family, your community, and the world. Spend time getting to know that great person of who you are.

After you have spent whatever time is necessary for you to get to know yourself, I would then challenge you to either write or type out a private journal on the thoughts you had regarding the questions asked. As a result of your reflection, did you get to know yourself any better? Did you learn anything new about yourself, and how will that further information help you in your journey to becoming the best rendition of yourself? By getting to know yourself better, you not only recognize the inspirations that may come your way, but equally as important, you will now be able to understand their value to the degree that it will enhance your Faith, Trust, and Confidence in who you are and the exciting destiny that is awaiting you.

Once you have completed this assignment, you are then invited to return to where you left off and resume reading.

Understanding the Person We Think We Know

We now move onto the second part of our equation which consist of understanding our selves and why we do what we do. In the context of our discussion, let's once again refresh our mind on the definition of the difference between first *knowing* our self as one side of the coin, and understanding our self as the other.

To oversimplify our answer, I will use myself as the example. As I stated earlier, my wife and I have been married for over 50 years. I

---

[13] Chapter VIII of Confessions of Saint Augustine

think I can say with a degree of comfort that I know who she is as a person. Over the past 50 years I have learned a lot of essential facts about her. For example; I am aware of the day she celebrates her birthday and her age. I know her level of education and the schools she attended. I think I also understand her habits and have a good idea of what she enjoys doing and what excites her. I have also learned her dislikes, her pet-peeves, and what frustrates her the most. I also know her religious beliefs as well as where she stands politically. However, even with all that knowledge that I am sure I know about her, I cannot tell you how many times I have admitted to having a problem with understanding her. But guess what, I doubt very much if I am alone on that. In fact, my wife has often said the same about me. People who are in a relationship, regardless of how strong it is, have been saying this about each other from the dawn of creation.

So yes, there is a difference between knowing yourself and understanding yourself. So again, while the "knowing" yourself can be considered as the "what" and "who" you are, the "understanding" yourself can be identified as the "why" you do what you do. The following points will provide a good basis as a starting point for a self-examination on getting to understand yourself and what makes you do, and act or react the way you do. This is the "why."

Are you an introvert or an extrovert?

Although the dictionary defines the word introvert as being a person who does not find it easy to talk to other people, whereas they define extrovert as being a person who is the exact opposite. Such a person likes being with and socializing with others. In other words, it could be said that an extrovert is more of an outgoing person, whereas an introvert is a person who tends to keep more to themselves.

If we dig deeper into their meaning however, we find that an introvert is more than merely a person who finds it difficult to talk to other people. Psychologist often state that an introvert is reenergized by getting away from the crowd and the hustle and bustle and pressure of everyday life. An introvert would take solace in retreating to a quiet place by themselves. An introvert is reenergized by sitting quietly on the beach reading a book, listening to music, and enjoying the peace and the relaxation of the natural surroundings.

On the other hand, an extrovert is a person who is reenergized by doing just the opposite. People and activities are how an extrovert is recharged. An extrovert is rejuvenated by playing a hard-fought game of volleyball, football or other contact sport. An extrovert finds their energy being with people, and sometimes the larger and more active they are with the crowd, the more reenergized they become.

That is not to imply that an introvert does not enjoy, or even need the interaction of others, nor that an extrovert doesn't enjoy and even need at times a quite peaceful time and place to relax. The point is to arrive at an understanding and knowledge of ourselves.

So, in the context of that definition, you are asked again "do you find yourself more as an introvert or an extrovert." At the end of a long week do you enjoy having a cocktail in the quiet peaceful atmosphere of your back patio, or are you more apt to go to a nightclub?

As a rule, most of us feel that to be a success it's essential to be an extrovert, after all, it's the extrovert who's good with people; it's the extrovert who is fun to be around; it's the extrovert who is assertive and willing to get out in front to lead. But remember our definition of both the introvert and extrovert as defining where reenergization of both mind and energy is found.

One would be shocked to learn how many well-known and highly successful people throughout history identify themselves as an introvert. For example, Warren Buffett is known as one of the most successful introverts and businessmen in the world. According to Buffett, when he started, he had the "intellect for business," but he felt he had to enroll in Dale Carnegie's, "How to Win Friends and Influence People," course because he didn't have a business persona. In other words, he thought of himself as too much of an introvert.

Steven Spielberg, one of the most successful, wealthiest, and influential personalities in Hollywood admitted as much and said he would prefer to spend time getting lost into movies.

Sheryl Sandberg, a senior executive with Facebook, told *The New York Times* in 2010 that Mark Zuckerberg, Facebook's founder and CEO, "is shy and introverted and he often does not seem very warm to people who don't know him, but he is warm."

And the list goes on to include folks like Michael Jordan, Meryl Streep, and Steve Wozniak to mention just a few.

A number of years ago my wife and I purchased a Houseboat on the Mississippi River. The marina in which we had our boat docked had over 150 slips and as a rule were filled to capacity each season. Most of the boats in the marina were in the general size of 40 ft. or larger and were owned by professionals from a variety of professions.

When we first purchased it, I envisioned getting to know the other boaters and becoming social friends, with evening dock parties every weekend. It wasn't long before we found this not to be the case. While we did meet and become friends with those docked around us, for the most part we found that most of the boaters wished to keep to themselves. It was not unusual to see folks get on their boat on a Friday afternoon, leave the dock and not return until sometime on Sunday.

What I discovered was that for many, the very reason why they were attracted to boating was so they could get away from everything. It provided them the opportunity to leave their professional lives behind for a just a day or so and recharge for the week that lies ahead.

It was not unusual to see a houseboat, or a large cruiser anchored out in some secluded back water for an entire weekend.

Understanding how you are best re-energized can be an essential step in understanding why you do what you do. So often people fail to successfully reenergize themselves because they are searching in the wrong place. Without reenergizing our mind, body, and the very soul of our being, the journey of our career, life, and ultimate destiny will be greatly impaired.

What is your tolerance level for risk?

Risk-taking is a relative term. One person may view a risk as a matter of everyday life, whereas the next person, engaging in the same degree of risk, would consider it as walking on the edge of the cliff of life. To truly understand ourselves we also need to have it somewhat clear in our minds as to what our comfort level is when it comes to risk-taking.

An excellent place to start with this assessment is to arrive at a definition as to how you would define a risk. Until one can understand what risk means to them, it may be impossible to also determine their comfort level. Having a clear understanding of your definition of risk and your comfort level with it, is an essential step of genuinely understanding not only Why you act or react to events in life, but maybe even more important are the situations that would be best for you to avoid.

For example, if I determine that my comfort level of risk is high, I may have no problem with taking on a new venture and traveling down uncharted waters. On the other hand, if I have a low tolerance of risk, it would be foolish for me to leave the security of my current steady job for a new and an unproven endeavor. Regardless of how qualified I may be to take on the new venture, due to my low tolerance of risk, sense of doubt, and worry may be more than I can tolerate.

Your Magnetic Energy

Understanding myself and my definition of risk will help me to make wise decisions as to not only what I do, but also why I should not do it.

What motivates you?

What is it that causes you to wring your hands with excitement and anticipation? What is it that gets your heart pumping with excitement? What is it that makes you emotionally excited and determined to move mountains?

Understanding what motivates us can be the key to us moving forward in life. Without motivation, we often permit life to pass us by. Proper motivation can be the fuel necessary to propel us into action.

But understanding the importance of motivation is one thing, realizing what it is that motivates us as individuals is quite something different. For example, in business, it is often automatically assumed that people are motivated by money. While this may be the case for some, for others, recognition of either accomplishments or their abilities may be more of a motivator.

In doing some soul searching we must ask ourselves, "In my personal life, am I motivated more by a desire to do something for someone, simply for the sake of doing a good deed that can provide a level of self-satisfaction, or am I more motivated by doing something for someone due to the rewards I hope to gain as a result of what I do?"

Motivation is the catalyst that can spur us into action. However, while the what that motivates us is important, we must also understand the why of our motivation. By having a better understanding of the what and why of our motivation is yet another key that helps us to better understand why we may enthusiastically embrace one idea while giving little or no thought or action to the next.

In Chapter Five it was discussed that our success is often determined by what we do with that period of time between receiving an Inspiration, to when it fades into obscurity. Often the difference between action or no-action can be determined by what our motivation is. Motivation that spurs us into action is another offspring of our Positive Thinking. But before our motivation will move us into action, it must be grounded in the foundation of Faith, Trust, and Confidence. The degree of which we are motivated into action is usually in direct proportion to the degree of emotional passion the motivation generates. It's this passion that causes us to wring our hands with excitement and anticipation.

Understanding both your strength and weaknesses

In this discussion, there's no right or wrong answer. It's only wrong when we fail to have a clear understanding of, or when we ignore, what our strengths and weaknesses are. Having a factual knowledge of and taking ownership of each will take some serious soul searching.

First, we must not consider our strengths as areas where we can stick out our chest and boast of how good we are. But in the same tone, it is also not wise that we view our weakness as deficiencies or downfalls that we should be ashamed of.

Each of us were created with our own specific strengths and weaknesses. We neither chose the strengths we have, nor did we make a mistake by placing a checkmark in front of and choosing our weakness. Think of the most gifted genius, or the most successful person you can imagine, and I can almost guarantee that person would give almost anything to have that one strength that you have of which they are lacking. The chances are they also could list one or more weakness they possess, a weakness that you would thank God that you do not have.

Let's face it; there's not a human alive who does not have specific strengths they can offer as well as certain deficiencies that they must rely on others to pick up where they are lacking. That's where the connectedness that we discussed earlier comes into play. That is why we were created to live and work together as a community. That is how we build upon each other's strength, of which also results in us becoming our best rendition in building the foundation of Faith, Trust, and Confidence that will inspire us to attain the destiny we were created for.

So, your challenge is to make a list of what you feel are your greatest strengths, as well as the specific areas you feel as your weakness. Now, let's go one step further and have your spouse or trusted friend make a similar list as to what they see as both your strength and weakness. Then compare notes.

Although it is not unusual for the two lists to coincide rather closely, at times the differences may shine a light on an area of strength that you may not have considered before. It may be this one area, that if further developed could prove to be your greatest asset in moving forward.

In your professional life, having a clear understanding of both your strength and weakness can provide the critical answer as to who you should be teaming up with to most effectively accomplish your objective. If your entire team consist of folks who have the same strengths as you, that still leaves your area of weakness as a void. To be successful at your objective, with the intent on becoming your best rendition and bring the most to your community, it is necessary that all bases are covered, this takes the talents of those possessing the strengths that you may be lacking.

At a conference, several years ago, this very issue was being discussed. During a break period, an individual shared with me his experience of how this very situation almost ruined his company. He said that he was now the president of a regional franchised motel chain. He shared the business was started by his father over 40 years ago. He said, "I grew up in the business. During my high school days, I cleaned rooms, mowed grass, and helped with maintenance. During summer breaks of my college days I worked as a front desk clerk. He said after graduation he went to work for the company and held a number of positions as he worked his way up to take the reins from his dad when he retired. He said, "When dad retired so too did several of the top people who had worked for him. So, I found the need to hire my own staff." He stated, "This is where the problem came in. When interviewing people, I focused on those who were like me. People who thought like me. People who had the same views of life as I did. I wasn't looking for the preverbal 'yes man,' but I did want those who shared my way of thinking as to how things should be run in the business."

He continued, "slowly over about three years. I had a total turnover of my top management staff. After several years, we began to experience some downturns in business. Our expansions were not on the same course as we had experienced in the past. Our properties did not appear to be as sharp and crisp as they were when Dad was running things. And to magnify things, our financial statements were beginning to suffer as well.

He finally hired a professional consultant to review their operations with the hopes some light could be shed on what they were doing that was causing them to slip. He said, "After two weeks of working hand in hand with my staff, the consultant met with me and reported his findings."

While the consultant had several suggestions, by far, the most glaring issue he reported was, "Your entire senior staff consists of a reflection of you. You have no one thinking or proposing anything different from what you already have in your mind." The consultant informed him that he had no one on his staff that was filling in the gaps. Everyone was running in the same lane. Everyone had the basic personality strengths, and no one was filling in the areas of weaknesses.

Our personal life is no different. The best relationships are those where the parties can work as a team. Where one lacks the other makes up. One person's weakness is the other person's strength, and the utilization of both of their assets and talents is what makes the relationship a success. Relationships that are in trouble often view their differences as what divides them, rather than how their differences should be complementing each other. Their differences are what makes them a true team that can work together to accomplish what others may view as the impossible.

Having a clear understanding of our strengths and weaknesses is an essential step in not only getting to know ourselves better, but also how best to utilize the assets we have at our disposal to build a solid foundation to become the best version of ourselves.

Do you embrace rules or do you rebel against them?

The answer to this question may reveal a lot about you to yourself. If you say that you typically embrace and follow the rules made by others, does that mean that you are a follower, or does it imply more that you are a team player? It may indicate that you cherish a peaceful co-existence, and by following the rules to the letter is a way for you to do your part to maintain that peace.

On the flip side of that coin, would you say that you typically rebel against rules, and is one who tends to look outside of the box to get things done. If so, this may say that your personality is one that instead of marching in perfect formation with the drill Sargent calling cadence, that you are more apt to follow the leader who gives the command of "charge" and then going full force ahead to accomplish the objective in whatever way that gets the job done. But then again it may also indicate that you feel, for one reason or another that you are better than everyone else, therefore the rules do not apply to you.

The reality is that there is a time and place for the need to both following or not following rules. Without rules, you can have chaos. Rules provide the boundaries for order, ethics, professionalism, and clear lines of expectations. Rules help to make sure that everyone is on the same page and provides the line of the should and should nots, and the can's and the must nots.

On the other hand, although rules should not be intentionally broken out of willful spite, rules at times must be re-evaluated to accommodate changing times and circumstances.

The key to understanding ourselves is not the rules themselves, but instead our attitude toward them. Often, if we dig deep enough, we may discover that our viewpoint and reaction to rules can be traced to an event of our past. But as was made clear in Chapter Three, our history does not mandate our future. We do have the ability to make the decision to change; we just need to elect to do so.

By having a clearer understanding of our personality as to how we relate to rules and regulations provides us a better understanding of where a more balanced demeanor may be warranted. Again, this can be an essential step in our understanding of why we do what we do, and the impact this can have in both our professional and personal life. The attitude we have about rules can have a direct impact on our journey and our quest to become our best rendition.

Are you a morning person or a night person?

So, in the context of our overall discussion, why is it important to understand if you are a morning person or a right person. Simply put, it will not only tell a lot as to the time of day when you are most creative and do your best work, but it will also help to understanding the time of the day you should avoid, when being at your best is important.

Again, permit me to use myself as an example: I am a morning person. I am usually out of bed by 5 or 5:30 at the latest. I have learned a long time ago that I do my best thinking, and in my best and most positive mood in the morning. Prior to retirement from business, I typically liked to arrive at the office by 6 AM so I could get my day off to the right start. But come 5:30 or 6 in the evening any creativity in my brain was fast shutting down. Come 7:00 or 8:00 at night the creative part of my brain turns into mush. Even to this day, if I am preparing for a keynote address or other task that requires my full creative attention, if I attempt to work after 6 or 7 PM, I will usually find that the majority of the time I will spend looking at the blank screens with very little creativity.

With this understanding, I plan my day so I am working during the hours that I am the most creative and productive. I schedule my most difficult meeting for earlier in the day when I am at my best, both creatively as well as my mood and temperament.

It is the rare individual who can always be at peak performance, regardless of the time of day. Understanding this fundamental aspect of ourselves permits us to arrange our day and our schedules so we can take advantage of our most creative and productive time, thus allowing us to accomplish the most toward becoming our best rendition.

What would you be willing to lie about and why?

Whether we want to admit it or not, but we all have certain aspects of our life that we would just as soon that not everyone would know about. Let's face it, some aspects of our lives are private and not the business of everyone else.

Although the question, "What would you l e about and why?" is far too strong, as lying about anything never prcduces anything good, it does drive home the point of where we would draw that line. What lengths are we willing to go to conceal who we are to others. Where is that line of where we call privacy? Where is that line where we can reveal too many of our warts and blemishes, to the point that it can become detrimental to us? Or, where also is that line of where we are making everything too much about our self ard thus become more boasting with the intent of building ourselves up with the true desire and hope of trying to cover up our true self?

Having a better understanding of where we draw those lines will help us to understand ourselves and thus make better decisions as a result.

Do you say yes (or no)too often?

If I am a person who says "yes" to every request, I'm most likely doing an injustice to not only myself but others as well. Sometimes it's important that we check our motivation as to why we say "yes" to everything. Are we saying yes because we are wanting to help whenever we can? Or are we saying yes because of our desire to please everyone, thus becoming the martyr? O⁻, are we really saying yes because we are afraid we will miss out on something?

If I consistently say yes to the boss, regardless of any consideration of what I already have on my plate, or my ability to complete the requested task, chances are that sooner or later I will be letting her down due to my inability to follow through with the requested work.

On the other hand, if I say "no" too often, the chances are I will gain the reputation of being uncooperative, self-centered with my time, or uncaring. Of which once again I'm doing an injustice to both myself and others. If I consistently say no to many of the boss's requests, I will soon be viewed as someone that cannot be relied upon to help.

Your Magnetic Energy

Here to we need to check our motivation as to why we tend to say no.

The key is a balance. On one side, if our personality is that of trying to be too much of a people pleaser without consideration of what we are already facing, we will sooner or later get ourselves into trouble by taking on more than we can handle. If we say no too many times, we will become insignificant or unreliable. Striving for balance should be our goal, but that goal will never be reached until we first arrive at a correct understanding of which side of the coin we typically land. Again. this ties into both our personality as well as what our true motivation is for saying yes or no. This may take some serious reflection as to when and why you say yes or no.

If money was no object, how would you fill your days and what would you do?

I always chuckle to myself whenever I hear someone say, "If I ever won the lottery I would continue with my present life and lifestyle and even keep the job I now have." Ya, right! While that would be the ideal thought, I think anyone would be a very rare individual who would not have a considerable change in their life and lifestyle. And as far as keeping their current job, well there is an outside chance that could happen, but I would imagine that at times you would be a bit more challenging for the boss to deal with.

Although none of us know how we would fill our days if money were no object, it is good to think about it. Not necessarily from the point that it can be fun to dream of the life of luxury and leisure we could possibly have, but more so, by giving this question serious thought it can go a long way to determine where our priorities lie.

After all the trips you always wanted to take were taken, and after you had your fill of playing golf or going fishing, how then would you fill your days. Would you spend your days and weeks manicuring your yard, or would you find yourself volunteering at the local soup kitchen or other social agency?

If you give this question serious thought and are honest with your answer, it may provide some good insight as to your understanding of yourself and where your priorities lie. It may provide a better understanding of your purpose and the mark you can make on this world. It may provide an understanding of why the foundation you had built for your life thus far, is now enabling you to become your VERY BEST version of yourself.

Understanding the "Why" of each of our goals.

For a person to go through life without goals is like a ship that's wandering aimlessly throughout the high seas. It may always be on the move, but it has no identified destination. Because its target destination is not known, it will also not know when it arrives, or if it is even docked in the right harbor.

While I am a firm proponent of having well-identified goals that are in writing and committed to, in the context of our discussion here my purpose is not to provide instructions on the proper method of setting goals, nor making a convincing argument on the importance of having goals. Instead, the focus of this discussion centers on having a clear and honest understanding of the "why" we have the goals that we do.

Having a goal of obtaining the next plateau in our career may be a very honorable and worthy goal. It may also be an essential step in our journey toward becoming our best rendition, but equally as important as the goal itself is an understanding of why we have that goal. If our primary motivation to accomplish that goal is only to pad our pockets with more money or to stroke our ego, that may say one thing about us. However, if we are motivated by our desire to better utilize our talents and become our best rendition, that will say something altogether different.

Your Magnetic Energy

Regardless of what our goals are, it's vital that we take the time to analyze our motivation and desire to attain that goal. Having a clear understanding of our goals and why they are important to us will help us to gain further insight into understanding ourselves. Armed with an honest discernment can maybe cause us to reevaluate one specific goal, and instead, focus our energy toward other goals that more accurately defines who we are.

Assignment

Having a clear understanding of ourselves is equally as important as it is to know our self. The best-selling author and corporate trainer Brian Tracy put it this way, "Self-acceptance begins in infancy, with the influence of your parents and siblings and other important people. Your level of self-acceptance is determined largely by how well you feel the important people in your life accept you. Your attitude toward yourself is determined largely by the attitudes that you think other people have toward you. When you believe that other people think highly of you, your level of self-acceptance and self-esteem goes straight up. The best way to build a healthy personality involves understanding yourself and your feelings."

Because the understanding we have of our self is so critical to our becoming our best rendition, I am inviting you to once again put down the book for a minimum of 24 hours, or longer if needed. Then repeat the same exercise as you did in getting to know yourself. I challenge you to pray about, meditate, or deliberate (again whatever fits your personality) on the ten questions just asked. After spending the time necessary, I invite you to either write or type out a personal journal on the conclusion you may have arrived at on each of the above sub-sections. This will again help you to have a better understanding of yourself. This new understanding may help you to make more sense as to not only what you do, but even more so why you may do some of the things you do? This new understanding of yourself can assist you in better understanding the paradigm that you have formed for your life, provide a better insight as to how you can use this renewed understanding to move forward in your journey to become your best version of yourself.

To Thyself Be True

Now that we have spent the necessary time and effort in our attempt to get to know and understand ourselves better, we now turn our discussion to the importance of remaining true to the person that we know ourselves to be.

Being true to yourself is not always an easy task, especially in this "need to be politically correct" society we live in today. Instead, it's a life-long practice that requires commitment and re-commitment, moment to moment, and day by day, as you grow in who you are and evolve into the best version of yourself. The answer to what is right for you always exists at the core of who you are, provided you give yourself space and time to listen.

When you are true to yourself, you will find yourself completely honest with who you are and the core values that define you. It also means that you are not willing to compromise your thoughts, feelings, and values only to appease the opinion of others. Although we may not have the right to impose our views and values on others, we do have every right to take a firm position on the principles and values we stand for.

To accurately know your true self and express it authentically, you first need to cultivate a deep and trusting relationship with yourself. Ultimately, this begins with an awareness of your inner most private thoughts and how you interact with the world you live in.

In the same way that no one can love another until they first love themselves, so to you cannot be true to anyone else until you are first true to yourself. This not only allows your individuality and uniqueness to shine through but, even as important, you find that you have a sense of comfort and satisfaction with your individuality and uniqueness.

To best accomplish this objective, the following points are offered as a basis from which to begin a focus toward remaining true to the true self we have discovered ourselves to be.

Don't hide your character or preferences

There's seldom very little to be gained by deceiving others about who you are or the values that define you. People who are true to themselves are comfortable with letting their true beliefs and personality be known without being overbearing. If you feel like you need to conceal parts of your character (including religious or political beliefs), it's possible that you're not true to yourself. That does not imply that you should find it necessity to stand on the soapbox and be vocally defensive or offensive regarding your beliefs. It merely means that to remain true to yourself you do not have to compromise what you believe by pacifying someone else. The determination on how firm and hard of a stand you take on an issue depends on not only the subject but also on the situation.

A good analogy that I often use is to decide, "is this a hill I am willing to die for, or do I choose to fight a more important battle on another day." Not all issues carry the same weight, but that does not mean we cannot remain true to our self, regardless of its weight. There are those times when the best way we can stay true to ourselves is merely agreeing to disagree.

Set boundaries with your time and space.

Above it was mentioned that in our desire to please others we often become a modern-day martyr. There is probably no other area where this can be the case than how we set the boundaries for our time and space.

For most of us, regardless of our path in life, we are finding ourselves going from morning till night. After spending 50 or more hours a week at work, plus running the kids from one event to another, trying to meet obligations to church, civic, or community events, not to mention the need to care of elderly parents or extended family, when all is said and done it can be challenging to find even a small amount of time for ourselves.

Sometimes due to all that we have on our plate, not only is it hard to find that alone time, but on those rare occasions when we do, it is easy to develop a bit of a guilt complex. Sometimes it can be difficult for us to believe and feel that it's okay to be alone; thus, the martyr syndrome comes into play. After enduring weeks and sometimes even months of these hard-fought schedules and commitment we can become almost resentful. This then leads to those guilt feelings, especially when you harbor those resentful feelings toward those very people who are most important to you in your life.

We need to face reality, time and space for relaxation and reflection is an absolute necessity for us all. If you're always busy giving your time and space to others, you'll never grow yourself. Remember from Chapter Two when it was pointed out that if you wish to be more and receive more, then you must first become more. In the same fashion, you will also never be able to give more until you first become more yourself.

By refusing to take time and space for yourself, you're doing everyone else a disservice by giving them a tired, unfocused, and stagnant version of yourself, that self that is often involved in their own little pity-party. Under those circumstances, you can never become more, and for sure not give more. Much less being true to yourself.

Your Magnetic Energy

Are you your real self when at work?

If you're like many professionals, you may feel like there's more than just the one of you. There's the you who wears a suit and attends meetings. There is the you who knows how to manage people and how to keep focused so to get things done. Or you're the accountant who puts on a serious persona to both clients and co-workers. Or maybe you're the nurse or the physician who is dealing with serious life and death issues day in and day out and does not feel that you can permit your true personal self to be known.

But that tide may be changing a bit in professional circles. Although a professional demeanor must always be adhered to and maintain that line of privacy for a personal life, that does not prohibit us from remaining true to ourselves. The attitude of "Be yourself" is the defining career advice from many counselors. It's heard everywhere from business leaders in the boardroom to graduation day speeches. It's also becoming a more common hiring tool that is used by HR departments with the hopes of attracting the best candidates.

Corporate image consultant and author David A. McKnight[14] believes that the best way to project and maintain an effective executive image is to bring at least part of yourself to the table. He offers several compelling reasons why this could be to your advantage, which includes:

- People won't follow you if they don't know who you are.
- As a fake you will make clients and customers uncomfortable.
- An honest workplace is a more effective workplace.
- You'll find out sooner if there's a bad match
- You'll connect better with customers.

In addition to the five points cited above, it goes without saying

---

[14] *The Zen of Executive Presence:* ©2013 By David A. McKnight, DAMstyle, Inc.

that if you incorporate your true self into your professional life that you are more likely to remain true to the total person that you are. Staying true to yourself in your professional life as well as your personal life will not only make your journey more meaningful, but it will also permit you to become your best rendition. Trying to be a different person with each hat we wear is a balancing act that is seldom maintained over the long haul and will never result in becoming our best rendition.

Be Steadfast with you principles and monitor your values

More than anything else, your principles and values will define who you are and what you are made of. Our best rendition and how true we are to ourselves will be predicated on how well we live our lives in accordance with the principles that define our true nature.

In his book, *Principle-Centered Leadership*, author and corporate consultant Dr. Stephen Covey defines principles in this way:

"Correct principles are like compasses: they are always pointing the way. And if we know how to read them, we won't get lost, confused, or fooled by different voices and values. Principles are self-evident, self-validating natural laws. They don't change or shift. They provide the 'true north' direction to our lives when navigating the 'streams' of our environments. Principles apply at all time in all places. They surface in the form of values, ideas, norms, and teachings that uplift, ennoble, fulfill, empower, and inspire people." [15]

As Dr. Covey states, our principles are fixed based on the ideas, norms, and teachings that molded us into the person we are today. Principles encompass that built-in sense of right and wrong that is a part of our human nature. For example, I do not need a law passed

---

[15] *Principle-Centered Leadership*, 1990, 1991 by Stephen R. Covey. First electronic edition published 2009 by Rosetta Books LLC, New York.

by Congress to tell me that it is dreadfully wrong to commit a mass shooting. The very nature of our humanity places a high value on life; therefore, this is one of the principles that can be defined as being self-evident and a self-validating natural law.

Other principles, however, are ingrained into our being by the teaching, encouragement, and coaching from our parents and teachers as well as those that we received from our faith and religious upbringing. As Covey states, "our principles are fixed and apply in all times and all places."

Our values, on the other hand, are not quite as solidly fixed as our principles. Covey further states this about values.

Values are subjective and internal. Values are like maps. Maps are not the territories; they are only subjective attempts to describe or represent the territory. The more closely our values or maps are aligned with correct principles—with the realities of the territory, with things as they are—the more accurate and useful they will be. However, when the territory is continually changing, when markets are continually shifting, any map is soon obsolete. A value-based map may provide some useful description, but the principle-centered compass provides invaluable vision and direction.[16]

As such, our values can be somewhat fluid since they tend to sometimes change to best adapt to whatever society's latest fad of political correctness may be. Although our basic principles may have held stable for generations, consider how many of our fundamental values have changed.

For example, consider the type of programming and permissiveness that is aired on network tv during prime time today compared to that of say even 40 years ago. Could that be viewed as a change in our value system?

[16] Ibid

Consider the perception of marriage today compared to just a few generations back. Could that be considered as a change in our value system, and would one or both examples be viewed as a diversion from our core principles?

But just because our values are changeable does not always mean they are all on a decline. Consider our current perception of equality and respect we owe to each other regardless of race, color, sex or creed. Most would agree, these are areas whereby our value system has advanced for the better. In the case of this example, most would also view this as realigning more to our core principles.

Our values also guide our interests and behaviors, so it's worth taking some time to figure out what they are. In the changing world we live in, although our values may change over time, the point is to check in with yourself and the clarity of your values to determine how they align with your principles.

My point here is not to suggest what anyone's principles should be, or the value system that anyone should adhere to. Instead, it's that we all must examine closely to determine if our values have drifted off course from the principles that define our true nature of who we are as an individual.

The only way we can hope to remain true to ourselves is when we follow the course as dictated by the principles that are ingrained into us by either the nature of our humanity or a stable upbringing by our parents and the religious and spiritual beliefs we have adopted. Adding to that is our perception of our value system and how they align with our principles. The complete definition of who we are as our true self will always be dictated by our decisions, actions, and attitudes that follow the principles and values we hold to be important.

9

Failure Is Not Fatal

Another important mindset that every person who has had a degree of sustained success understands is, regardless of the amount of positive magnetic energy we generate, regardless of all the inspiring thoughts that may come our way, sometimes due to the simple fact of the nature of our humanity and the world we live in, we can and do make mistakes.

Not only do we make mistakes, but sometimes the reality is such that we are just out of sync with the universe. Sometimes life itself refuses to cooperate with us and our plans.

In Chapter Seven, I shared the story of my good friend who experienced the pain and devastation of a heartbreaking divorce. This was far from the plans he envisioned for himself and his family.

I can also assure you that in my business career, the impact of several of my setbacks and financial losses did not line up with the business plan and the future I had planned.

Let's face it; sometimes life has a way of just happening. It's not always a walk in the park, and as I already said, that is a reality of our humanity and the world we live in.

However, the one thing that people who have experienced success have deeply ingrained into their mindset is that regardless of how we may define it, and irrespective of its size or nature, *failure is never fatal.*

One would be hard-pressed to find any successful person who has not met with numerous failures or at lease significant setbacks in his or her lifetime, whether it be in their career or their personal life.

For example, did you know that prior to starting the Ford Motor Company, Henry Ford had failed in all his previous business ventures? It is said that he went broke five times.

Walt Disney was once fired as a newspaper editor and was told that he lacked imagination and had no good ideas.

Oprah Winfrey was once fired from her job as a television reporter and was told that she was unfit for TV. I can imagine that on the day she was fired, and as she sat alone in her small apartment, she considered herself a total failure. To her at that moment, she felt that her whole world, along with all her hopes and dreams had suddenly all come to an end.

Michael Jordan once stated, "I've missed more than 9,000 shots in my career. I've lost almost 300 games. Twenty-six times I've been trusted to take the game winning shot and missed. I've failed over and over and over again in my life. And that is why I succeeded." [17]

Can you imagine what would have ultimately happened to Michael's career if each time that he failed he had adopted the mindset that he was a failure at the game of basketball? Can you

---

[17] *100 Inspirational Quotes* by Michael F. Bolle, 2017

imagine how different the world would be if Walt Disney or Oprah Winfrey had accepted the opinion of others? What if Henry Ford had resigned himself to the idea that he was not good at business, therefore after losing three or four times he would be foolish to try again? What if any of these people would have considered their failure as fatal and therefore blocked out or discarded all future inspirations they received toward becoming all that they had within their ability to become.

At a given point, each of these individuals had to make the conscious decision to turn the page and begin life anew by regaining control. Each of these individuals had to realize that although they may have failed at a specific task at that specific time of their life's journey, yet they as a person, with the freedom and ability to think and act, were not failures. They had to develop a mindset, a firm conviction that their situation did not define who they were, or equally as important; their situation would not define who they could or would become. They had to decide that the situation would not become their flee trainer with the glass jar.

Each of these individuals faced circumstances that, for the most part, were totally out of their control. Going forward they had one of two choices to make.

One option would be to curl up in a fetal position and blame the world or someone else for the situation they found themselves in, and then take the path of the least resistance by giving up and quit trying.

The second option, which successful people have adopted as their mindset, is to understand that one's past, or even the present, only becomes a detriment to one's future if we permit it to do so.

That's not to minimize the pain that any failure or significant setback can cause. However, after a "reasonable" period of time to lick one's wounds, and if necessary even to grieve one's loss, successful people make the conscious decision to pick themselves up, dust themselves off, and do whatever is required to reenergize their positive magnetic energy so as to once again generate the positive thinking that will get their Inspirations to flow their way, so they can regain control and head down that path toward their desired destiny in life.

Consider the life story of J.K Rowling who today is considered as one of the wealthiest and most influential authors in Great Britain. But that is not by far who she always was. There was a time in her life in which she was a self-proclaimed failure. She was a divorced, bankrupt single parent living on welfare. Even though she was at the lowest point of her life, still she maintained enough positive energy to act upon the inspiration she had to begin writing a children's book. For her, it was an inspiration that she was determined to follow through with.

When completed she sent the manuscript to dozens of publishers, and each sent her letters of rejection. Her journey took a turn to the positive when Bloomsbury Publishing House in London agreed to publish the manuscript directly on the bases that the publisher asked his eight-year-old daughter to read the first chapter and immediately she demanded to read the rest of the book. But even Bloomsbury had advised her not to give up her day job as it was almost impossible for an author to earn enough from a single children's book.

Oh yes! I forgot to mention that the title of her book was *Harry Potter*. The rest, as we know is history. The Harry Potter series has won multiple awards, translated into over 80 languages and sold over 400 million copies! They have been the basis of a series of *Harry Potter* films as well. The *Harry Potter* books have been bestsellers and gained recognition for sparking an interest in reading among the young at a time when children were thought to be abandoning books for computers and television.

In June of 2008, she was invited to deliver the commencement address to the graduating class at Harvard University. She told the class, "*Failure meant a stripping away of the inessential. I stopped pretending to myself that I was anything other than what I was and began to direct all my energy to finish the only work that mattered to me. Had I succeeded at anything else, I might never have found the determination to succeed in the one area where I truly belonged. I was set free, because my greatest fear had been realized, and I was still alive, and I still had a daughter whom I adored, and I had an old typewriter and a big idea. And so rock bottom became a solid foundation on which I rebuilt my life.*" She concluded by saying, "*What I feared most for myself at your age was not poverty, but failure.*"

Although I have not achieved the level of success and notoriety as that of J.K Rowling, yet I can empathize with her experience of failure.

For me, one of the times I experienced what I interpreted as a major failure in my life all began on October 6, 1979. But first, let me set the stage. As I stated in my introduction, I entered the Real Estate profession in 1972. Through hard work, long hours and determination I experienced what was viewed by many as an above-average success. Within a few short years I progressed from a salesperson to a Broker Owner. By the mid '70s the company had grown to a staff of over 35 salespeople, plus a top-notch office support staff.

By the late 70s we were well on our way to becoming a force to be reckoned with in our market area. We felt unstoppable. But then things changed.

To combat the runaway inflation that our Nation had been experiencing, of which by the way, in the first nine months of 1979 inflation was at an annualized rate of 10.75%. So, on October 6, 1979, the then Federal Reserve Chairman Paul Volker initiated a policy that raised the Federal Discount Rate that amounted to an unprecedented four percentage points in a single month, of which culminated at the end of the month at 15.5%. Compare that to the current rate of today of being less than 3%.

Prior to this event, interest rates on a typical 30-year fixed-rate mortgage was in the general range of 10 to 10.5%. By April of 1980, only six months later, mortgage rates were running well over 16%. Add to that the unemployment rate reached 9% by the end of 1979.

So, needless to say, Real Estate sales went down the tubes. And as sales went so went our company. While in the short tenure of the company, we experienced substantial success, yet we did not have the benefit of longevity to establish a foundation to withstand the impact of the devastating change in both the market and consumer demands.

Ok, enough fluff of rationality. The bottom line was that we were of the mindset of, "things are great, and they will never change." With that mindset, we focused 100% on growth and nothing on establishing a foundation. So, guess what, over the next year, regardless of our efforts, the bleeding wouldn't stop. I finally had no other options but to surrender and start over. The company we had worked so hard to grow to its level of success, was now gone.

After I locked the office door for the last time, I spent the next six months grieving my loss. A significant factor in my grief was that I was wadding in the mud of believing that I was the failure.

Finally, a trusted mentor threw me a lifeline. He explained the reality of the world we live in. He assured me that life did not come with a written money back warranty. Sometimes life just happens, and when it does the best we can do is to make sure we take good notes on the lesson we learned, hopefully not to repeat them. He told me I had a decision to make. He challenged me as to if I was willing to take advantage of that education, learn and grow from it, or I would rather throw it away and let the event define my future?

I did take good notes, sometimes maybe they were not as good as I should have, but like J.K. Rowling so appropriately put it, I used my rock bottom to form a solid foundation to build my life and my future. A future that almost 30 years later permitted me to retire as the President and /CEO of a multi-million-dollar company.

So, if you have ever had the experience of failing at anything in life, don't feel that you are alone. You should consider yourself as being in excellent company, as most everyone has failed, to one degree or another, at one thing or another. Be assured you are in a big club with the rest of us.

It's now your turn to be honest with yourself. I invite you to think of a situation in your life that you can describe as being a failure or a major setback.

Maybe this was in a business or other professional venture or position that went south.

Maybe it was more personal, such as a broken relationship.

Maybe it was a financial loss due to an investment gone wrong.

I can almost guarantee that there are very few of us, if any, who have experienced any amount of life whatsoever, who have not felt the pain of failure or a significant setback in one form or another.

As you reflect on the events of your life, I invite you to note in the space provided below a brief description of whatever that one failure or setback that tends to haunt you the most, or at least that one that you tend to think about most often. _____

_____

_____

_____

_____.

Now I would ask that you ponder on that for a moment, and then ask yourself, "How has this loss, setback or self-described failure played a role in how I define myself as to who I am today?" Has that situation crippled me to the point that I cannot move forward? Has it made me almost too cautious or even hesitant to move forward by accepting the value and validity of the positive inspiration that comes my way?

Or has it lit a fire in my belly to motivate me to regain control once again and move forward in my journey leading me to my desired destiny in life? How have you used your failure or set back to strengthen the foundation that has given you the courage to move forward?

Earlier, in Chapter One, during our discussion on the definition of success, you made a list of ten or more times in your life in which you considered yourself a success. I invite you to carefully review your list once again. Once you have absorbed your list of successes, then return here to continue reading.

If you do the math and divide that number 1c (*the number of times you were successful*) by the number 11, (*which equates to the total number of our ten success and one failure*) it means that you are the winner almost 91% of the time! Bearing in mind both your success and your one self-described failure, I would now invite you to reflect upon the impact that your one identified loss or failure had in the way you are now defining who you are.

Why is it that even though we can be the winner most of the time, (say 91% or better) yet so often we let that one loss be the deciding definition as to how we describe and identify ourselves?

As difficult as it may be at times, what separates the successful people from the mediocre people of the world, is the mindset they have as to how they handle failure and setbacks, and the ultimate effect they permit it to have in their lives. J.K Rowling is also attributing to saying, *"It is impossible to live without failing at something unless you live so cautiously that you might as well not have lived at all—in which case, you fail by default."*

We have all heard the statement many times, *"It is not what happens to us in life that matters; rather, it is how we handle what happens to us that matters."*

The successful person has the mindset that success cannot always be 100% guaranteed. They understand there is always that degree of risk for the possibility of failure or a significant setback. But to such a person, if failure does happen, regaining control and moving forward again is the only option.

I am sure that most of us did not have to think too long before we could identify that loss that we may have considered as being almost catastrophic. However, do you realize that the losses that have the most devastating impact on our destiny are not those that we may consider as being the catastrophic mistake or failure? Instead, it's usually those little everyday losses, disappointments, and rejections that our mind soon convinces our brain that we are just no good at, whatever that may be. Our mind tells our brain that we tried, but we can't do it, so why not just admit that we are a failure, especially in that specific area of endeavor. Therefore, why should we keep trying?

That first airplane would have never left the ground without the consideration of some element of the possibility of a crash, and history tells us there were many crashes.

Yet how often, when a salesperson "crashes" in his attempts at prospecting, or fails to close a sale, does he consider himself a failure? He either leaves the business or settles for a mediocre career by picking only the easy low-hanging fruit. Think about it, what effect does this fear of failure have on such a person's career and ultimate destiny?

What about the corporate person who applies for an advanced position within the company but doesn't get the job? Then six months to a year later applies for another advancement position, but again loses out and doesn't get it. Often, after only two attempts, the mind tells the brain that the pain of rejection is just too great, and after all, there is no chance of ever being chosen for an advanced position. Fear of rejection and failure sets in, and we become our own flea trainer. So, the decision is made never to risk the chance of hitting the head against that jar lid again. Once again, consider the impact this fear of rejection and failure can have on one's career, not to mention the ultimate destiny.

Alan Shepard, John Glenn, or any of our other first astronauts would have never enjoyed the ticker tape parade if there was not that distinct possibility of failure that they had to overcome.

The ticker tape parades each one of us will enjoy will be in direct proportion to how we can overcome our fear of failure. Remember, regardless of how large we may envision that obstacle to be: *Failure is not fatal.*

Successful people view failure and or setbacks as their inability to achieve a specific task or plan on a specific date and moment in their history. On the other hand, unsuccessful or mediocre people often will take failure personally and equate their inability to achieve their objective more as to who they are as a person, and therefore consider *themselves* as the failure. Often these little failures become the obituary that defines the ultimate destiny of their life and career.

These two diverse thought processes create two different mindsets and eventual outcomes.

One looks at the "task" as being tried and unsuccessful, whereas the other looks at "themselves" as trying and failing. One looks at failure as an event, whereas the other looks upon themselves, as a person, as the failure. The mindset they possess will determine the control they elect to take over their futures.

People like Oprah, Ford, Disney, or the millions upon millions of other very successful people in all walks of life could never have become the person they eventually did had they permitted their failures to be the final obituary that would define their destiny.

Overcoming Fear of Failure

To have the same mindset as that of successful people who enjoy their ticker tape parade every day, we need to consider how we can overcome our fear of failure. I challenge you to consider the following:

First, it's essential that we understand and believe that following any failure or setback, through a constant generation of positive magnetic energy and regaining a positive attitude toward life, it will always - always attract the right positive flow of Inspiration into our life that will present new and exciting opportunities. The more we regenerate positive magnetic energy with an attitude and a mindset of Positive Thinking that has the foundational blocks of Faith, Trust, and Confidence, the more likely we will be able to make those firm decisions and commitments to move forward once our new inspirational opportunities present themselves. Regardless of the area of our life that it may concern, the more we dwell on our failures or setbacks, the less likely that the Inspiration for new opportunities will ever come our way.

Recall the power of the magnet and how it will push away that which it does not like. Whenever we dwell on past mistakes, failures, or setbacks, our negative magnetic energy is in full power and will push away and suffocate any chance for the potential of positive inspiration for new opportunities.

Secondly, we need to propel our decisions and commitments into action. The longer we wait to act upon the Inspiration we receive, the more our fear and skepticism will increase. Confidence is never created as the result of dreaming, wishing, or hoping. Only our actions create momentum; momentum builds confidence; and the more confidence we have, the more our fear and skepticism will be reduced and eliminated; thus, the more positive magnetic energy we will generate.

Positive Thinking < Inspiration + Confidence + Action = Success

Whenever we permit fear of failure to hold us back we become our own flea trainer. We choose to set our own limits. If we are sincere about becoming our best rendition, we must take ownership of our decisions and the path we have chosen. If we do, just accepting that responsibility will go a long way in taking or retaking full control of the destiny of our career and our life.

Now that we have our foundation in place, going forward in the next few chapters, we will be discussing several concepts, ideas, and practices that will assist you in making those decisions to gain the control that may be missing in your career and life.

Communication

There was a time in our history when the primary method humans had to communicate with each other was through voice communication. In other words, people actually talked to each other. Wow! What a novel and creative idea that was!

Then as a society, we advanced and began communicating through the written word. This occurred through the various methods of written correspondence such as letters, newspapers, and so on.

We advanced even further, and our mode of communication was improved with the invention of the telegram and the telephone. This gave us the ability to communicate almost instantly over long distances.

Then the voice mailbox came onto the scene and we were told we would never again miss an important message and our ability to communicate would improve.

Soon to follow, the fax machine was invented. This gave us an instant transfer of letters, contracts, or other written documents, allowing for almost immediate communication of our written correspondence.

We continued our advancement and soon everyone had a cell phone. Suddenly we discovered that we could communicate with anyone regardless of whether we were in our car, in the office, at home on our back deck having a cocktail or a glass of wine, or even somewhere in a duck blind out in the wilderness.

Then somewhere along the line the Internet came into our lives. With the added new feature of email, we were offered yet another way for us to communicate.

Then came the Blackberry, and soon to follow the smartphones came onto the scene. These phones provided the technology of not only the ability of texting, but we could also receive our emails, plus Twitter, Facebook, and a host of other social media outlets.

Guess what? We have now advanced to the point where we have all these tools that allow us to communicate with each other, yet even with all the technology, instead of improving communication, we have made it worse. It seems that we now have less direct communication with each other than we have had at almost any time during recent history.

The other day I pulled up at a stoplight and happened notice the passengers in the car next to me. There were four teenagers in the car. Each had a cell phone, and each was texting. From my vantage point, there was no communication, much less direct communication occurring among these four teens.

But let's not pick on the just the teens. How often do we also see adult couples at a restaurant, a time that could be a precious one-on-one time spent with each other, yet doing the same as the four kids in the car?

In my opinion, our communication with each other as human beings has never been as lackadaisical as it is today. Too often direct communication is viewed as being not only as unimportant but in too many instances it is even deemed as unnecessary.

Our lack of communication, rather let me rephrase that, the failure for proper and meaningful communication is becoming more and more of an issue that is having a less than a favorable impact on virtually every aspect of our life, our relationships, our society, and yes even our economy.

Consider the limited level of communication that most of us have in our personal lives. Although we may think we are in constant communication with our spouse and children by way of our texting and other forms of modern-day technology, yet the reality is such that meaningful and truly effective communication with our loved ones is seldom accomplished by the texting of one or two sentences. Not to mention that it is impossible to express any degree of emotion in what we are saying.

But this negative impact of our lack of communication does not stop with our personal life. The reality is such that this issue is also harming our professional life and it can be downright bad for business.

These days it seems to be a common occurrence to hear businesspeople in virtually every profession complain about the lack of loyalty that exists. This lack of loyalty does not stop with customers and clients, but it has also well infiltrated the ranks of both employers and employees.

There was a day when it was a well-understood fact that *people primarily did business with people and only secondarily with the business entity or a company.* It was well understood that it was the company's job to make the phone ring or bring the customer or client to the door, yet it was the people within the company that made the cash register ring by the service they provided to the customer.

The loyalty a customer or client has to the company is always directly attributed to the degree of commitment they have to the person, that human being that they are conducting their business with.

How can we expect to develop any sense of loyalty with a customer or client when there is so very little, or even no direct communication between two human beings? How can we expect any degree of loyalty from another human being when there is little or no human relationship ever established, much less maintained between the parties?

We live in a very competitive world. Consider for a minute how many of your competitors are selling the same product or provide the same service as you do, and at or close to the general competitive price as yours. In so many instances that which provides the competitive advantage is most often due to the relationships that is built and maintained.

It is only when a stable relationship exists that we can even hope to build a sustainable base of customers and clients who will remain loyal to us. Having reliable products, competitive pricing, and a solid company is all vitally important. But ultimately, it will be the relationship between two human beings that will establish and maintain long-term loyalty.

It frustrates me to no end when I am trying to do business with someone and find so many people who seldom answer their phone. Although they do leave a message on their voice mail, yet in so many instances, they seldom return a call, rather they send a text. So, then I text them, then they text me back, and so on. What can take 30 to 40 minutes or longer at times to complete the communication could have been done in less than five minutes by talking to each other over the phone. But the time element is only part of the problem, the most critical issue is that no human contact was made. No relationship is established or maintained. Now maybe that's my age showing through, yet it is usually that same person who I hear complaining that they receive no loyalty from their customers or clients.

The same scenario exists between an employer and its employees. People work for people, not for institutions or corporations. It's always a two-way street. Loyalty only exists between people. So, if more loyalty is desired, it is then necessary that a relationship must be established, and a good relationship can seldom exist without proper communication between two human beings.

Effective Communication = Loyalty

But the importance of good communication does not stop with the issue of loyalty. Anyone in business today knows all too well how easy it is to find yourself in the middle of litigation or a contentious problem or issue. In every aspect of life, one of the best ways to reduce the potential of a lawsuit or a festering problem is to have a better line of communication between all the parties. As human beings, simply talking to each other can often move mountains when attempting to resolve problems and issues.

But people just are not doing so. Often, they permit their communication, or lack thereof, to deteriorate to the point that the only remaining option is to let the attorneys do the talking for them.

Effective Communication = Successful Resolution

An important ingredient in the foundation of the mindset for successful people is their understanding that in one way or another every problem will ultimately come to a final resolution. It may not always be according to our liking, but it will always come to a final resolution. Successful people face the problem or issue head-on. They don't wait until it's out of control, rather they move in early with an attempt to take as much control as possible through prompt, proper, and sincere communication.

When a complaint letter lands on their desk, it becomes a priority to be addressed. Complaint calls are either taken or returned with a sense of urgency. The successful person understands the reality that delaying communication will only heighten the irritation and magnify the issue or situation to the point that it gets out of control. The sooner the issues is defused, the less likely it will be to blow up.

President Theodore Roosevelt is quoted as saying, *"I don't care how much you know until I know how much you care."* [18] Whenever authentic care and concern is conveyed through positive communication with an honest desire to find a resolution, most often the festering will stop, and at least some sense of control to resolve the problem is maintained.

If any of us really think back to some of the problems or issues we may have had to deal with in the past, regardless if it was of a personal or professional concern, we will usually discover that the issues we were able to resolve the easiest and the fastest were those in which proper and positive communication was established early on and then moved to make every effort to address it as soon as possible. The sooner we move in to tackle a problem with open and positive communication the more manageable it will remain.

However, good business dictates that the fear of litigation should not be the primary motivation for excellent and open communication. The primary motivator should be our desire to maintain stable customer/client relationships.

---

[18] This quote is believed to have originated in a June 1900 letter from Theodore Roosevelt to Mark Hanna but no known source can be found to verify the attribution. https://www.theodorerooseveltcenter.org/Learn-About-TR/TR-Quotes?page=3

Your Magnetic Energy

I am always amazed at the number of companies and business professionals who will spend considerably more time, money, and effort in trying to get a new customer than they will in keeping existing one.

While watching television during prime time, (6 PM to 10 PM), it's not unusual, especially when watching one of the primary network stations, that we can be exposed to upwards of 50 commercials. For the fun of it, try keeping track of the number of ads that are directed more toward getting a new customer versus those focusing on maintaining an existing customer. This occurs even though experience overwhelming proves that the longer a customer or client is with a company, the more loyal they become. Not to mention the fact that every professional is well aware that the longer a positive relationship is maintained with a customer or client, the more likely they will also send more business to the firm by way of referrals and recommendations.

Without a doubt, sound business practices along with delivering a good product or service at a fair and completive price are always necessary. That should be assumed as a given, as most of your competitors are striving for the same thing. A solid customer base will most likely be maintained when a stable relationship exists. Having proper and ongoing personal, one on one communication with your clients is one of the best ways to keep a relationship that translates into loyalty.

Of all the modern-day methods we have available for one to one communication with each other, I think it would be safe to say that the four primary ways that are used most often consist of texting, email, phone conversations, and personal face-to-face communications. Each one of these fulfills an essential need. The key, however, is to understand the *why* and *when* to use each to achieve their proper purpose.

If a solid relationship is desired, then consider this comparison. Which news reporter do you typically feel most connected to, the newspaper reporter, the radio reporter, or the TV reporter? Although I don't have any statistical back-up, I would think it would be safe to say that overwhelmingly most people would feel most connected to the TV reporter, then the radio reporter, with the newspaper reporter coming in last. I draw this conclusion primarily due to the type of personal contact that we psychologically have with the person. Because we can see their face, their expressions, and other body languages we tend to identify easiest with the television reporter. The next is a radio reporter. Because we can hear the tone and expressions of their voice, we tend to feel a connection.

We tend to feel the least connection with the newspaper reporter, simply because we not only can't see or hear their voice. Additionally, and unfortunately for them, the majority of the time we read the article without even looking at the reporter's name.

Now relate that same scenario to receiving either a text message, a phone call, or having a face-to-face meeting with someone. While each has their place, it's the face-to-face conversation in which we can build the most meaningful relationship, and when that's not possible a person-to-person phone conversation is the next best.

If we hope to maintain control over any aspect of our life, we must be perceived as being a master at communication. Members of both political parties often consider both President John F. Kennedy and President Ronald Reagan as being effective presidents, not only because they were wise or strong leaders, but even more so because of their ability to be an effective and persuasive communicator.

The more effective our communication skills become, the greater chance we will have in controlling the destiny of our career and life. Our ability to build a solid foundation toward becoming our best rendition will so often be tied directly to our ability to communicate effectively with others. If you feel you are lacking in this area, I encourage you to read some of the many good books or take a class at your local community college on the art of effective communications. You will find that the dividends will reward you greatly.

11

Time Management

Calculating Its Value

If I made the statement to you, "I want to hire you to manage a department within my company." Or, "It's about time that you begin to manage your finances." What impression would come into your mind from each of these statements?

Naturally, the tone and the context from which I would be making those statements would play a part in the impression you'd get. But I think that it would be safe to say that when I use the word "manage" what I am really saying is that I want you to "take control" of whatever it is that I want you to "manage" so that the outcome will be more favorable

However, when the words "time management" are mentioned, we tend to get somewhat of a negative connotation from it. We so often get the immediate impression that someone is going to tell us what to do or how we should be spending our time so that we can do more work in the time we have.

If that's your impression of the subject of "time management," let me put your mind at ease. Numerous times throughout this chapter I will repeat the statement, *"What you do with your time is entirely up to you."* This chapter is not about telling you how you should be spending your time; it is about giving you suggestions as to how you can control it instead of letting your time control you.

The more we study the lives and actions of successful people, regardless of the profession they may be in, the more we will find how they value their time. And the more they value their time, the more they have mastered the art of taking control of their lives.

TIME MANAGEMENT = CONTROL = SUCCESS

As a result of their ability to master the management and control of their time, this permits them to accomplish more and be more so they can ultimately bring more to the table.

With better control of our time, we typically will experience less stress, which leads to also providing an additional bonus of more enjoyment of what can be often described as a higher quality of life, all of which leads to a higher degree of fulfillment and satisfaction that we seek in our quest for success.

While some things in life are totally outside of our control, how we manage and control our time is one of the few things that is virtually 100% within our control.

Because we so often fail to admit to this fact, let me repeat what I just said so that you keep it better planted in your mind, *"How we manage our time is one of the few things that is virtually 100% within our control."*

Understanding the degree of control we have over our time is of vital importance. The less control we have, the higher the chances are that time will control us. It's just this simple: the first critical step in having any degree of control over our career, our life, and thus our ultimate destiny is that we must first master the art of controlling our time.

We live in a day and age when time seems to be at an absolute premium. Because life, schedules, commitments, and responsibilities are all demanding more and more of our time each day, it is not unusual for one to conclude that effective time management sometimes can boil down to a matter of controlling the chaos of daily life. While it may be true that controlling chaos is an important step in managing our lives, yet it goes beyond that. Therefore, lets continue our discussion with a consideration of just how much control we do have over our time. I invite you to consider your answers to the following few questions.

Do you have the *ability* to say the word "No"? If you do, then you have control over how you will spend your time.

When the alarm goes off in the morning, do you have the *ability* to hit the snooze button, or even turn the alarm clock off? Now understand this, I did not ask if you had the luxury, instead I asked if you had the ability. If you do, then you have control over how you will spend your time.

Do you have the *ability* to elect not to go to work today? Once again, I asked if you had the ability, not the luxury. If you do, then you have control over your time.

The list of such questions could go on and on. Regardless of how you answered each of these three questions, the correct answer to each is "Yes." Yes, you do have the ability to say "no" regardless of the request or who may be making it. Yes, you do have the ability to keep pushing that snooze button as many times as you wish, and yes you also can elect not to go to work today or any other day.

However, while the ability may exist, the ramifications of our actions may not always be as we want, or it may come at a higher price than we are willing or wanting to pay. Therefore, the real function of time management is to give us the ability to control and utilize our time in a way that is in our very best interest.

Pushing the snooze button so many times that it makes me late for work may not be using my time in what may be in my best interest. On the other hand, pushing that snooze button or even turning it off on a Saturday following a rough and hectic week may be by far the highest and best use of my time, and yes, even being in my very best interest.

Time management is about using our time most efficiently and effectively so that it is in our best interest, thus permitting us to grow closer to the success that we desire. Time management is about helping to make the journey more manageable. What it all boils down to is that time management is not about managing time, it is 100% about the management of what we do during a given period that will prove to be in our highest and best interest. But that is sometimes a lot easier to say than it is to live out in this hectic world.

As mentioned earlier, we live in a day and age where time is a commodity that is at an absolute premium. Not only are most of us running from morning until night, but the absolute travesty is that at the end of the day a lot of us not only wonder where the day had gone, but we often find ourselves scratching our heads and wondering just what we had accomplished.

The fact is each of us have only 24 hours in a single day. Time is a fixed commodity for each one of us. None of us can make or create more time in our life. But we *do* have 100% control over what we do and how we spend every one of those 24 hours that each day provides to us.

How we spend our time will naturally result in what we can productively accomplish during those 24 hours. What we accomplish during each 24 hours will determine either the growth or the stagnation of our career, our life, and our journey toward our desired destiny. How we spend our time will determine both the quality of our own life, as well as both the quality and quantity of what we can give of ourselves to our loved ones. Our best rendition will be largely predicated on what it is that we do during each 24-hour period of time that we are given.

Ask yourself: While at work, am I more prone to spend my time with a focus on accomplishing the mission of the company, or do I spend my time with mindless busywork that will ease my guilt with the appearance of being busy, yet accomplishing very little?

When I spend time with friends or family, am I present to them or is my attention divided between them and the text I am receiving or replying to?

If you recall, earlier I mentioned that so often it's the little changes in life that can make a dramatic difference. The ability to manage your time, both effectively and efficiently, is again one of those areas that will provide you with just such a winning edge that you need to succeed toward becoming your best rendition.

It's the employee who is focused on accomplishing the objective for which she was hired, or the parent who is intent on hearing, learning, and responding to how their child's day went, these are the folks who will find themselves on the winning edge. Again, it's often the little things that can make a dramatic difference in the destiny of one's life.

By implementing the suggestions discussed in this chapter, most readers will experience a *minimum of a 15 to 20% increase* in the efficiency of what they can accomplish with their time.

So often in life, it can be a that 15 to 20% that will make the difference between a high degree of success or that of mediocrity or stagnation in any area of life.

Think of this for a minute: If you had a 15 to 20% increase in efficiency, that would mean that you would have an extra 15 to 20% more time available to you.

Understand this. I'm not saying that I will show you how to do 15 to 20% more work in the time you have. Efficiency is not a matter of just doing more. Instead, it's a matter of doing what we already do, but doing it in less time, thus having more time left over. It's totally up to you to decide what you will do with that extra time. In like manner, efficiency is also not about working harder. Efficiency is about controlling what you do with the time you have to accomplish what is most important to you. Efficiency is about making the travel of our journey not only smoother but equally as important, permitting us to smell the roses along the way.

Visualize it in this manner. Say that you have an objective that you need to accomplish in a specific block of time. Say your time allotment for accomplishing your task is five hours. So that means that under your current mode of operation, the objective you must achieve will take the entire five hours to complete. Now imagine if you could accomplish that same objective in only four hours. That would leave you one full hour remaining. That remaining one hour represents a 20% increase in efficiency. Hypothetically, that would be one full hour that you could redeem in whatever way you desired.

What would it mean if you could continue to do exactly what you're doing today and at the same pace, with a continued focus on a high quality of output, and yet at the end of each day you had an extra one hour that remained unused? Again, remember that these one-hour blocks of time would be available for you to redeem and use in any way that you desired.

Also consider this: The average person spends approximately 50 hours per week at work these days. Using the example above, when applying the same scenario to a 50-hour week, do you realize that 20% equates to the equivalent of an extra 10 hours a week? That is an additional 10 hours per week that can be used for yet a higher quality of your productive output, *assuming that is what you want to do with it*. From that perspective alone, that 10 hours per week translates into over 500 hours per year, which mathematically translates into the equivalent of an extra ten weeks of productive value that you can bring to your career. From a purely economic standpoint, that is an extra ten weeks per year of additional productive output that you bring to the table. But again, what you do with that extra ten weeks per year is entirely up to you.

But now, also try this on for size. Say your income is derived from either a salary or other type of level wage, How much more valuable would you be to your employer if you could bring an extra 10 hours per week of productive time to the table? And the real bonus is, that's *without* working any harder or adding more stress to your life. Remember also that we are still working with our initial 50-hour work week. We are not adding any more time to your day or week. Those ten extra hours of productive time consists of those 10 hours we had accumulated due to our increased efficiency.

Let's look at it from another realistic-life perspective. Because you have become the master of what you do with your time, how much more valuable would you be to your employer if your productive output was 15 to 20% greater than what is typical of your co-workers?

On the other hand, if you're an individual who works on an incentive or commission-based income, how much more revenue could you generate if you had an opportunity to be productive an extra 10 hours per week, and again this is without working harder or investing more time. As mentioned above, ten hours per week represents a 20% increase in efficiency. What impact would a 20% increase in efficiency make for your bottom line? I invite you to do the math as it applies to your income. Now be honest, does that increase in income warrant serious consideration of the application of proper time management? For that matter, what if it amounted to only a 10% increase, would it still be worth serious consideration?

But the productive value and added income we may receive because of the effective management of our time represents only the tangible monetary value, which is not to be overlooked.

The intangible value lies in the self-fulfillment we receive on our journey as a result of the confidence and satisfaction that we gain due to our ability to get the job done not only on time but ahead of time. Not to mention the satisfaction of knowing that we had accomplished our objective by getting it done right the first time. This does not even take into consideration how much smoother and more of a relaxed pace that our life will seem to run when we are not always behind the preverbal eight ball by trying to beat the clock, or worse yet, needing to catch the clock.

The added value is that we can do the same amount of work but do it in less time, or at a minimum at a more relaxed pace. This results in deadlines becoming more manageable, which also equates to less stress. In addition, because we are less hurried the likelihood of common mistakes are also significantly reduced.

Over the years psychologists and time management experts have done considerable study and research on the importance of having a focused control of how we spend our time. Without question, most of these studies indicate that *the more control we have over what it is that we do with our time, the more control we will have over all aspects of our life and thus our destiny.*

The more responsibility we accept for what it is that we do with our time, the more we energize our positive magnetic energy, which will attract even more Inspired positive opportunities into our life. Only by controlling what we do with our time will we also take control and implement the Inspiration that comes our way. Without that, we permit our inspirational thoughts and ideas to pass us by like diamonds floating down the stream.

Ten Principles

As already stated, to master time management is to master what we do with the time we have available. To do this best there are ten proven principles that we must understand if we wish to achieve peak performance.

These ten principles are recognized by almost everyone who has achieved sustainable success. Successful people have further developed these principles as an integral part of the foundation of their mindset.

These ten principles will assist in generating the positive magnetic energy we need to attract greater inspiration for opportunities into every area of our life. The more opportunities we have available to us, the higher our potential to become our best possible rendition.

Principle 1. *The more we can control and manage what we do with our time, the greater the contribution we will make; thus, the greater the value of what we bring to the table.*

Regardless of whether it involves our profession, our families, or our social life, the value of our contribution will be directly tied to the quality of the time we can devote to it. The more success you experience in all areas of your life, the higher the need you will have for better control of your time. Therefore, if advancement or improvement in any area of your life is on your agenda, then having better control of how you spend your time will be an aspect that you will not only *want* to learn how to master, but it will be imperative, as your chances of success will be significantly reduced when your time controls you instead of you controlling your time.

There is no question. There can be no debate. Almost all the critical factors of success rely on proper time management.

We have all experienced the frustration of working with or doing business with someone who has poor time management skills. Years ago, there was a sign posted outside a cubical at our local City Building Department that read, *"Your inability to manage your time properly is not what triggers our sense of urgency."* Isn't that so often the case? People who cannot manage their time correctly so often expect others to jump through hoops to accommodate what I call their irresponsibility or their lack of respect for my time.

A person with poor time management skills will seldom be considered for a leadership position. Those who cannot manage what they do with their own time will rarely have the ability to manage the time of anyone else. The ability to control and manage time is one of the primary traits of good leadership. There is no possible way for anyone, in any profession, regardless of the level of responsibility to become the best version of themselves if they fail to control and manage their time effectively.

Principle 2. *Professional productivity requires time.*

Ideally, the more time we have, the more we can produce. Looking at that another way is to say, the more control we have over our time, the more control we have over our productive value.

The value of one's productive output will always determine one of the main distinctions between people who have shown sustainable success, from that of people who perform at a fraction of what the top performers can bring to the table.

As it relates to our careers, effective time management requires that you continually ask yourself:

- Why exactly has the company hired me?
- What am I expected to accomplish, or what is it that I want to achieve in a day, a week, or a month?
- How much productive value do I bring to the table that will aid in accomplishing the objective or mission of the company?
- What is the highest degree, and best use of my time that will deliver the most value to what I am doing?

The more we focus on the output we deliver, the better and more effective we will become. This all relates to the control we have over our productive time.

Principle 3. *Everything you accomplish or fail to accomplish depends on your ability to use your time to its highest and best use.*

You can only increase the quality and quantity of your results by improving your ability to use your time more effectively.

Did you catch the essence of what I just stated? I didn't say that you can only increase the quality and quantity of your results by working harder. Instead, I said that the quality and quantity of your results will be based on your ability to use your time more effectively. Working hard is an assumption. That's not the issue as most people are not lazy and consequently do work hard.

Regardless of whether we get paid on commission, if we work for a salary, or if we get paid by the hour, our pay is never based on the time we spend at work. Instead, our compensation will always be predicated on whether we are delivering an increased value to the mission of the company. That is always based not just on time as measured by the clock, but rather on how we use our time most effectively to accomplish the objective.

Principle 4. *Time is often our most limited asset.*

In America today, a major problem most people are experiencing is time poverty. We are short of time in almost every area of our lives. Time is not elastic; it cannot be stretched. Time is indispensable; all work and all activities of life, including sleep and relaxation, demand it. Time is irreplaceable; there is no substitute for it. Time is perishable; it cannot be preserved, stored, or stockpiled. Once it is gone, it is gone forever.

Principle 5. *Judgment, foresight, discipline, and at times even our ethics can all go by the wayside when we become stressed due to the lack of the time needed to accomplish our required objective.*

The skillful management of time enables you to get things done correctly and without a high degree of stress.

My grandpa always told us, *"People are like lemons, when they are under pressure and squeezed, what they are made of is what will come out."*

When we feel the pressure of time, we feel squeezed the most. Proper time management will not only help reduce that pressure, but in many instances can even eliminate it.

Consider our 50-hour work week example from earlier. How much less stress and pressure would you experience if you could meet the deadline of your weekly assigned task or objective and still have the luxury of even five, much less ten hours remaining?

Chances are if you think about it, many, if not most of the stupid mistakes you have made in your life, or the important details you may have overlooked occurred at a time when you were pressed for time. The higher the pressure of time becomes, the more pressure and stress we experience. This all too often results in doing whatever is needed to get it off our plate. That may involve a rush to judgment, or maybe taking shortcuts, or just not taking the time to think things through. Regardless, seldom does this result in us becoming the best rendition of ourselves.

Principle 6. *The more we focus on the management of our time, the more result oriented we will become.*

Your ability to focus single-mindedly on the most significant results required of you is the fastest and most reliable way to get paid more, promoted faster, and achieve the rewards of the goals you are seeking.

Even in our personal and social relationships, time impacts the success and effectiveness of our relationships. The more quality time we spend with someone, the more our relationship will grow. That can only happen by the intentional devotion of our time.

Principle 7. *Time management enables you to work smarter not just harder.*

Do you realize that in virtually every industry or profession, most people who fall into the category of being mediocre tend to work just as hard and put in just as much time as the person with a higher degree of success? The problem is they only produce less in the hours they work because of their inability to manage what they do with their time effectively. Working smarter means using our time in a way that is in our best interest so we can accomplish the objective at hand.

Principle 8. *Good time management is a source of generating positive magnetic energy and inspiration.*

Proper time management can produce passion and a feeling of self-esteem into our journey. In turn, this enhanced self-esteem becomes a source of regeneration of our positive magnetic energy, which in turn attracts the Inspiration for even greater opportunities.

Proper time management also helps us to visualize the journey of achieving our goals with more clarity.

There is an old saying that says: "It's hard to remember that the initial objective was to drain the swamp when one is up to their ass in alligators." In the same manner, it is difficult to have clarity of the vision of our objective when we are being pushed, pressured, and stressed due to time restraints.

Principle 9. *Time management is a stress reducer.*

Although stress can be the result of many different issues in our lives, it cannot be denied that the more we lose control of what we do with our time, the more stress we will experience. As we discussed in Principle 8, it is almost impossible to keep in clear vision the journey we had planned when our mind is preoccupied by stress and anxiety due to the pressure of time.

When it comes to our daily work-related stress, think about the typical occasions in your life that causes you the most significant tension. As a rule, it's when you are running behind and trying to catch up. When such is the case, it can be easy to lose sight of the initial objective for which we set out to accomplish. The more frustration we experience, the more out of control we feel. Not to mention, the more critical time becomes is when we tend to make stupid mistakes or overlook important details, either of which can also cause additional stress and frustration.

Principle 10. *Effective time management begins with the minute you are currently living, for this is the only minute in which you have any control over what you do.*

The final and perhaps the most critical principle to grasp is this one. Past minutes are gone forever, and future minutes are only projections. We cannot do anything about the past. The only sure thing we can control is what we choose to do with this time, this exact moment we now have.

Procrastination is the number one enemy of time management. Procrastination is nothing but the regeneration of negative magnetic energy.

Now that we have discussed the importance of time management, and hopefully you are now convinced how critical it is to the control we have of, both who we are and who we wish to become, let's turn to several proven techniques that will provide the upper hand in managing what you can accomplish with your time.

The Toolbox

The management of how we best use our time consists of three primary objectives. The first is to develop a tactical plan. The second objective is to make the commitment, and the third is to create accountability. It will be these three objectives we will be building by using this primary tool in our toolbox.

When it comes to the ability to manage our time, the most vital tool that we have in our toolbox is that of our scheduling calendar. But before we go any further it is of absolute importance that we understand that our scheduling calendar is only a tool, an important one yes, but it is just a tool. As such we must always maintain the position that we are the master of our tools, we can never permit our tools to be the master of us. The minute we allow our scheduling calendar to be our master that is when we lose control.

With that said, I now invite you to take out your scheduling calendar. Regardless of the type you use, it could be the paper "Day-Timer™" or one of the "At a Glance™" books. Or it could be one of the many apps available on your phone, tablets, or computer. Regardless, the type or version you use is only secondary to the importance of your commitment to using it correctly.

First, mentally recall all you have on your plate for the next five to seven days. What are the priority items that you need to or want to accomplish during that time? What, if any, deadlines are you facing? Do you have any tasks or objectives in which you are running behind or have been putting off for another day? If so, what importance do they play in the overall goals you have for the next five to seven days?

Now that you have somewhat of a global perspective on the next five to seven days, compare that to what you have entered on your schedule, first for today and then tomorrow. As you review just those first two days, do the events you have already scheduled fall in line with the priorities you have established for the next five to seven days, or are you already off track?

Does your schedule for those first two days include everything that you need to or want to accomplish for both days, or are you keeping some of your commitments in your mind only, without entering it on your schedule?

Does your calendar clearly outline where you need to be and how you intend to spend your *entire* day?

Does your calendar also include those items that would typically be on a *To-Do* list? In other words, does your schedule include items that popped into your head of things you would like to do when and if you have time to get at them, but if you don't, it's not all that critical as you could do them another day?

To use our scheduling calendar effectively, it *must* be guarded as the tool that gives us optimal control of our entire day by providing the tactical map that we have *committed* ourselves to follow in order to maneuver the events of our day. Committing to the schedule that you have created is not surrendering to your calendar as the master. Instead, it's committing to what you need to do so that you can take control of and master what you do with your time as effectively and efficiently as possible.

Now I invite you to glance at the specific details of everything you have on your calendar for next week.

Have you scheduled *all* your standing appointments? When I say *all* standing appointments, I mean anything and everything that requires a commitment of your time. This includes all events from scheduled staff meetings, to picking up the kids at school, to the important meeting with a valued client.

This means everything from the time you have committed to jogging in the morning before work, your Rotary Club meeting at noon, and the dinner engagement with friends in the evening. Everything that requires a commitment of your time must be entered into your scheduling calendar, and every item entered must also have both a start and end time.

As we have already mentioned, one vital aspect of having effective control of one's time is that it greatly assists with reducing stress. This cannot be the case if you find yourself consistently running late to appointments and commitments. Therefore, it's critical that you not only schedule ample time for each task or appointment but that you also schedule the appropriate amount of time for either prep work or travel time.

When it comes to standing appointments, it's easy to give in to the temptation of having an attitude of, *"That's something I do every day, and I know from memory that I have to do it, so I don't need to write it down."*

When this temptation hits, remind yourself how many times you may have double booked yourself because you got busy and failed to remember what you thought for sure you had memorized. Why take the chance of not only double booking but also getting so busy that a commitment you made slips your mind? Likewise, if for example, you don't schedule a time to do things like jogging or working out, the chances are they won't get done.

I now invite you to scan your calendar for next week again and as you look at each day, determine whether you have any standing appointments that you have not entered on your calendar.

If you have just one standing appointment missing, that's the one that could throw off your entire day. Missing or arriving late for that one routine appointment could result in your single biggest regret of the week.

Now let's go back again to focus on your schedule for tomorrow. What does it look like? Does your calendar represent everything you want to or need to accomplish? Again, when I refer to *everything*, I mean just that—*everything*. Not only your appointments and commitments, but *everything* you have on your plate that you want to or need to accomplish tomorrow that will require a commitment of a block of your time and attention.

It is of utmost importance that every event that requires a commitment of your time is entered, and I cannot stress this enough, *you must enter it immediately, as soon as you elect to commit your time to it.*

Once it's entered, you no longer have a need to expend brain cells trying to recall what you committed yourself to do. If later it must be rescheduled to a different time or even different day because of a more pressing priority, then so be it. But even rescheduling it keeps it on the plate to complete at a given scheduled time in the future and eliminates the chances of you forgetting about it.

Developing a Tactical Plan

Now that you have all your appointments and commitments recorded on your scheduling calendar with both a start time and an end time, it is now time to devise a plan to get everything done. This begins when you come to the end of your workday. Here is where the first of our three primary objectives come into play as we develop our *"Tactical Plan."*

The first objective in developing our tactical plan is to establish a practice that every day before you shut down, however that is defined for you, you first review your scheduled appointments for the next workday from a global perspective. From this point of view, you can quickly determine what that next day will stack up to be. Does it keep in line with the priorities and objectives you have for the entire week?

Does your calendar indicate that you are booked solid from morning till night, or does it look quite empty with a lot of open times available?

Are there any appointments you have committed yourself to, or objectives you need to accomplish that you failed to enter on your calendar?

For those entries you have on your calendar, is the time scheduled both ample and realistic, and have you also included needed prep and travel time?

Once you have completed this global review, it's now time to complete your tactical plan by getting down to specifics.

To do this, you begin by determining if you have anything scheduled for the first thing in the morning. This not only will act as a reminder of what's in store and how hard you will need to hit the ground running tomorrow, but more importantly, it will also provide for ample time to prepare for whatever appointment, meetings, or commitment you may have.

Sometimes this may require taking work home so you're ready to go. To prepare for that early morning appointment, you could organize the files on your desk or in your brief case so you're ready to go. This can help to eliminate those last-minute stresses when you're hurrying the next morning as the client is waiting for you.

While your typical day may have many scheduled commitments, it is also not that unusual to have several unscheduled time slots, and that's not always a negative. It depends entirely on how we choose to use those time slots to our best advantage. Remember, you are the master of your time; make your time work for you.

Another critical point to remember. If those open time slots are not intentionally scheduled, chances are more than a few will get wasted or at a minimum they will be filled with busy work. Recall, the key word here is "control." You have the option to use the time as you feel is in your best interest. So again, if you do not intentionally schedule your time so it is used as you want, chances are the time will merely get wasted.

To prevent this from happening, as you review your schedule for tomorrow, you must take control over those free times by turning them into productive time. As the control is in your hands, so too is the definition of what "productive time" may mean to you on any specific day.

Consider your scheduling calendar in this way—if it's not scheduled, then you don't intend to do it. If you want to, need to, or plan to do it, then it must be on your calendar with both a starting and ending time. That even includes play time.

Our Commitment
Once we have completed both our global review and established

our tactical plan for tomorrow, we are now ready for the second of our primary objectives in our time-planning process. We now move on to Step #2, which is making a firm commitment to the tactical plan we have established.

Remember this important point: For any item you put on your scheduling calendar, you are committing to fulfill that item during the time slot you scheduled. You should never take the attitude that an item on your calendar is entered as a reminder. For example, say you make an entry that you need to pay a specific bill on the first day of the month. This entry should not be viewed as a simple reminder, but rather is a commitment to pay the bill, and because it requires time and attention, both the start and end time must be entered. It's critical that you must commit to both the objective and the time to accomplish it.

In other words, for this example, you would meet that commitment that you scheduled by actually writing the check and dropping it in the mail. If you do not fully intend to commit yourself to this objective of paying this bill, at this specific time then it should not be on your scheduling calendar, that's what a to-do reminder list is for. No entry on your scheduling calendar is ever made merely as a reminder, but instead it's a commitment to a call for action.

Of course, there is always a chance that pressing issues or other priorities could come up that will cause us to somewhat rearrange our day. However, even when that does happen, you're still the master, and as such you are in control to determine which issue should or must take precedence, and which will be scheduled for a different time.

Only by making a firm commitment to our tactical plan can we put our mind to rest for the day. Committing to our plan dramatically reduces the chances of forgetting something important. With this commitment in place we will significantly reduce those sleepless nights, worrying how we are going to get done all that we need to. Our plan will tell us in full detail exactly how we will successfully maneuver through the events of the day.

The Critical Path

Occasionally someone will ask, *"But I do the same thing all day long, how will a scheduling calendar help me to control my time or help me to be more efficient?"*

One of my staff architectural draftsman once made a very similar comment to me. He said when he begins working on a project; he works on nothing but that one project until he has completed it. He stated that a scheduling calendar for his daily work routine would be almost useless.

Keep in mind, regardless of the position we have or the job for which we are responsible, *every job* is time sensitive. There is no such thing as having a task where time is not a consideration. It is well known that every task has a way of filling up the time given to do it. Unless we assume the position of being the master of our time and take control of what we do with that time, it will get filled up with *something*, and often that *something*, can be the wrong *something* that can turn into the master of us.

So, this is how I instructed my draftsman. Say he's assigned a new project and is told the deadline for completion is 60 days from now. Unless he puts together a realistic critical path agenda that he can commit himself to follow throughout every day of his 60-day assignment, chances are he will find himself either burning the midnight candle during the last few days to meet the schedule, or he will fall behind and fail to meet the deadline.

A critical path agenda is merely breaking the big project down into smaller weekly, daily, and sometimes even hourly tasks with a time sensitive deadline for each.

In the case of my draftsman, he must first analyze the project so he can get the total overall scope pictured in his mind. He then breaks his overall task down into smaller tasks that he needs to accomplish to meet his final objective.

For example, he determines how much time it will take to do the site plan, the foundation, the structural building shell, the interior floorplan, finishes, and so on. With each item on his critical path, he has now put together a schedule that will tell him what he must accomplish each day to meet the deadline that he has committed himself to. If after completing the critical path agenda he discovers that the 60-day allotted time is not realistic, now is the time this should be addressed, not on the 55th day when he can see he needs to add at least another ten days to the original 60-day schedule.

Whether you're in accounting, marketing, product design and development, a support person, or a manager of people or procedures, controlling what you do with your time and meeting deadlines is critical to your success and the value you can bring to the table. How we schedule our time and our commitment to follow thru is a direct reflection as to our commitment to become our best rendition.

The Unexpected

Once you begin entering *everything* on your calendar, you will often find that your calendar is filled from early in the morning until late at night. If this is the case, I'm sure that you are often faced with the dilemma of how to handle the unexpected issues that come up, such as when that client or customer pops in unexpectedly, or when either your boss or a fellow employee needs some of your time. If you are already booked solid, it can throw your entire schedule into a tizzy.

Your Magnetic Energy

To address this problem, I have found that having a practice of blocking out 30 to 45 minutes right after lunch, and if possible, another 30 to 45 minutes at the end of the day can provide the leeway needed to maintain your sanity and still meet all your committed objectives.

For example, say today you are booked with non-stop appointments, but you had the wisdom to reserve these two open times slots. Say that someone approaches you during the morning and asked if you can spare some time for assistance on a project the person is working on. Or a client calls and says he need to meet with you right away. An effective way to handle such impromptu issues is to tell that person that you are pressed right now, but that you would have about 30 minutes at 1 o'clock if that would work. But then follow that by also asking if it's a pressing issue that needs to be addressed immediately. By doing so you are telling the person that you are willing to adjust to give them priority if needed. In most cases however, the reply will be, "One o'clock will work great," or he may simply say, "I only need five minutes. Can you do it right now?" Depending on current priorities, you handle it accordingly. The same is true when issues come up during the afternoon.

So why schedule this open time right after lunch and again at the end of the day? Why not mid-morning or mid-afternoon?

In my experience I have found that by doing it after lunch, quite often problems and or perceived priorities tend to lessen or even resolve themselves if given some time to percolate, therefore reducing the time it may take. As a rule, a high percentage of issues we face daily do not increase in severity within an hour or so.

Or why schedule a time at the end of the day? Interestingly enough, I have found that quite often things don't take near as long at closing time as they would during the middle of the day.

Not only does this provide a time slot for those impromptu

requests, but equally as important, when such requests do *not* come up, this then can provide an excellent opportunity as a catch-up time during both midday and at the end of the day for some of the items on your to-do reminder list. But again, you must take control of these time slots to make them productive.

If you find that impromptu interruptions are interfering with your daily schedule and continually throwing you off base, then by making these simple, but necessary corrections you should become at least another 4 to 6% efficient and productive with your day.

Skill, Behavior, and Habit

Time management and personal efficiency skills are disciplines that we learn with practice and repetition. Once these basic skills are understood, it is then that our individual behaviors and the everyday commitments we make regarding our time will determine our ability to maintain control and be the master of our time.

The best news is that if you practice top-notch time management religiously for just 90 days or so, most of those practices will develop into habits that will stay with you until you consciously decide to change. As previously stated, time management is a matter of skill and behavior. It's a matter of practice and repetition, both of which are always very much a matter of choice and control.

Every day, we make the conscious choice as to if we will use our time to become the best rendition of ourselves, or if we will allow life to pass us by. It is 100% our choice as to whether we want to become more efficient and take control of our time and our life, or if we want to accept things as they come, therefore permitting time or others to have the control and be the master of our destiny.

The more effective one becomes with the management of time, the more positive magnetic energy we will generate. When we have control of our time, it is then that we also can focus on, evaluate, and better implement the inspirations that come our way.

By making sure that every event or task you want to, intend to, or need to accomplish throughout the day is entered on your calendar, and then by filling in all uncommitted times with productive work or activities, that alone will provide for more than the 20% increase in productivity that we spoke of earlier.

Only when we control our time and become the Master of it can we even begin to have a chance to control and be the master of our careers, our life, and our destiny.

Return on Time Invested

As already mentioned, management of time is primarily determined by what we elect to do with our time. So, if what we do with our time is important, then another way to consider time management is to look at it in terms of a *"Return on Time Invested."*

As a Real Estate Developer, the primary emphasis of our business was to design, build and lease to either to single or multiple tenants. As such I was constantly evaluating projects based on the quality of the investment. One primary aspect of my evaluation was always based on its *"Risk vs. Return on Investment."*

Likewise, it's crucial for us to consider the same fundamental analysis when it comes to our time. After all, how we invest our time and the value of the return we receive will determine our ability to become the best rendition of ourselves that will permit us to make the journey necessary to obtain the success we desire.

The chances are that you have heard of the 80/20 theory that was introduced by the Italian economist Vilfredo Pareto. In the 1800s he arrived at the conclusion that the society of his day was divided into what he referred to as the "vital few" of which he described as the top 20% in terms of money and influence, and the "trivial many" that he referred to as the bottom 80%.[19] He later discovered that virtually all economic activities were subject to this principle as well.

This 80/20 theory has been studied and verified countless times over the past 200 plus years, and it can be applied to so many aspects of our lives. For example, his theory has shown that 20% of your customers will account for 80% of your sales. 20% of your products or services will account for 80% of your profits, to mention just a few instances where his theory has proven to be correct.

As it relates to the management of your time and what you do with your time, this rule states that 20% of your activities on any given day or week will account for 80% of your positive results, and further that 20% of the task that you take on will account for 80% of the value of what you do.

For most of us, if we were brutally honest and accurately analyze everything we do throughout the day, the chances are that we would also find that typically only 20% of our activities produce 80% of the value of what we accomplish.

Based on this 80/20 theory, if you look at your calendar over a period of a week's time, strictly in terms of value and return on time invested, chances are you will also discover that two out of ten of your scheduled tasks will produce greater value than the other eight do together.

Therefore, by focusing on these two tasks and doing them right, and right the first time, you would get the highest payoff of return from the investment of your time.

Considering this strictly from a job and career standpoint, as already mentioned several times, the reason for every job and the role of every person in every position is to add value to the mission

---

[19] The Pareto principle is named after the Italian economist Vilfredo Pareto (1848-1923)

of the company. The bottom line is, regardless of the job or position, if it cannot or does not add value to the mission of the company, the chances are it will soon be eliminated. In today's economy with fierce competition and slim margins, there are very few companies who have any of those so-called luxury positions. Most of those were eliminated and never returned following the Great Recession of the '80s.

Therefore, if your goal is to become more valuable to your organization, then begin by asking yourself, *"Of all the things that I do, where and how do I contribute the greatest value to my company?"* If you analyze your work carefully, you will find that there are usually only a few of all the activities you do throughout your week that will provide upwards to 80% or more of the value you contribute to your company.

To determine your strongest areas of contribution, begin with this question: *"If I could do only one thing all day long, what one activity would contribute the greatest value to my job, my career, or my business?"*

To become the most effective and the most productive at whatever task you have on your plate, it's vital that you always think in terms of both priority and where you will receive the highest return on time invested.

I challenge you to think about this 80/20 theory of time management carefully. The more focus you have on it, the higher you will find that your productive output will become.

But in doing so, that *does not* mean that you must automatically eliminate all those tasks that fall into that less productive category, as some of those are important for the overall success of the company, to your career, as well as life in general.

Let me give you a simple real-life example. My wife and I have six children. As they were growing up my first and primary responsibility as a parent was to spend quality time with them. Now if I compare the importance of spending time with my children to that of say, mowing the lawn, hands down the time I spend with my kids would by far rank as being in that top 20% of importance. However, mowing the grass was also important. Not as important as spending time with the kids, and yes may be considered as being in that bottom 80% of importance, yet needless to say, it was not a task I could eliminate. If I wanted to be a good neighbor, have a nice yard for the kids to play, and maintain my property value, I needed to mow the lawn.

Get the point? Not all less important tasks can be eliminated. There are numerous examples and times when those less-important tasks will become the building blocks for those all-important tasks. Some degree of common sense with an understanding of your job must come into play.

What this does mean, however, is that by having more of a focus on this 80/20 theory, we can eliminate some of the less productive tasks that can often be considered only "busy work." How much more of what we do could then be moved into the category of receiving a higher return on time invested?

If we do this, instead of being in a high productive state for only two hours a day, maybe we instead would be in that high productive mode for even two and a half or three hours of the day. That alone would mean we would add over a 25 to 30% increase in the overall value of what we accomplish. Ask yourself, what would that 25 to 30% increase mean to you, your company, and your career?

Time Audit

Another way that we can take better control of our time is by completing an accurate audit of how we are currently using our time.

Your Magnetic Energy

The more precise you are in your audit and your analysis of how you are spending your minutes and hours, the more accurate and effective you will become with what you do with your time.

Because most of us never perform this critical review, seldom are we aware of the amount of time that we waste every day of our lives. When I use the term waste, I am not referring to the fact that we may not be in our highest productive mode, but rather maybe we are not using our time for what is in our best interest. Sometimes, taking a break from the action and going for a walk to clear our mind would be very much in our best interest. So, our objective is to use our time to the highest and best use so that it is in our best interest.

Think of it this way. If I am having an issue with my finances and I'm finding it difficult to stretch my money through to the end of the month, what are two things I need to do?

Well, logic tells me that the first thing I must do is to come up with a workable budget. But there is one other important step I must take before any budget is workable. That step is, I must have a full understanding as to where I am now spending my money. I will never be able to get my finances under control unless and until I have a thorough understanding of where my money is now going. Only then can I determine with any degree of accuracy if I am spending my money in a way that is in my best interest.

The same is true with our time. We will never be able to control and budget our time unless we first have a full and clear understanding of where and how we are now spending it.

Over the years I have personally used two workable methods of auditing to determine what I was accomplishing with my time. Depending on your personal needs and how serious you are about getting a better control of your time, you may choose also to do both.

Audit Method #1

The first auditing method I used involves looking at my scheduling calendar for the past month. I would seriously study and honestly analyze each day.

- How many empty and open time slots were unaccounted for?
- Did my scheduling calendar provide an accurate history of my life during the past 30 days?
- Were there any meetings, appointments, or commitments that I either missed or was late for because I either didn't have it scheduled or did not have enough time scheduled?
- Were there any days that I felt pressured or rushed because I had so much on my plate for that day, yet in looking back now, my calendar for that specific day did not reflect it?
- Were there any days that I did not accomplish as much as I would have liked, and if so, what did my calendar look like for those days?
- Did my calendar include all my standing appointments, regardless of what they were for?
- Did it include both a start time and an end time for everything I had entered, and did the time I scheduled also include time for both preparation and travel?
- Did my scheduled appointments and commitments also include a brief note as to the purpose of each event?
- Did my calendar include both my professional and personal commitments?

Often as I would study and analyze the entries on my calendar, I would find that if I could redo my schedule it would definitely look different, and chances are I would have also been not only more productive, but my life would have run smoother.

Audit Method #2

The second method I have used was to keep a detailed personal log as to my activities throughout the day. Whereas my first audit would examine my past schedules, this examined my daily activities from a real time prospective. As such, this audit is performed by writing down everything I do throughout the day.

For this, I never use my scheduling calendar. Rather I would use a small pocket scheduling calendar that the Bank gave away as a premium item. I am sure today many will find a more appropriate electronic app in which your entries can be either typed or voice recorded.

Regardless of the tool used, it's vital that every activity throughout your day is recorded, and once again by everything, I mean everything.

If I spent an hour in a meeting—I record the time it started and the time it was finished. I also included the purpose of the meeting along with travel or prep time.

If someone made an unexpected stop into my office, I recorded it. And to repeat it once again, it's important that you record the time it started, the time it ended, and the reason that person stopped in.

The purpose of this audit is to provide you with valuable information as to the events that is consuming your time throughout your day. As such the accuracy of the information you receive will be in direct relation to the information you enter. Therefore, it's vital that everything that required any amount of your time is recorded, not only those that take 15 to 30 minutes or more but also those that take even five minutes. Let's face it, things always take more than the so-called five minutes. First, it breaks your concentration, which you need to reestablish, and second, seldom can anything be accomplished in five minutes.

Think of it in these terms: How accurate would my checkbook be if I said I only enter checks into the register that are over $5.00?

As with anything in life, so too with this audit, some common sense also needs to apply. Remember, your objective for this audit is for you to get a handle as to how your time is being consumed. It's not to justify anything to anyone else. So, your degree of honesty is only to yourself.

Another important key is that you must not change your routine during this audit period. The honesty and accuracy that you have with what you record will determine the value you get from the final analysis of this time audit.

At the end of each day, I could then evaluate if and how my time was spent in its highest and best use, and thus spent in a way that was in my best interest. The reality was that I often discovered that I needed to get a better handle on the way I was controlling my time.

But like that of any analysis or study, the information that it provides only becomes of value when it is acted upon. Therefore, once I completed the honest analysis of my time audit, I then had to discern what I could have done or should be doing to take better control of it and not allow it to control me.

Could I have accomplished the same objectives with greater efficiency by simply rearranging my schedule? Would that have made me more productive, less hurried, or more efficient?

I also wanted to take into consideration the 80/20 theory regarding my "Return on Time Invested." I often discovered that the real value was at the end of the week when I add up all the unproductive time, or the time I could have or should have been devoting to those two or three tasks that provided the highest return on time invested.

My audit would often bring to light just how much time I was spending doing the so called "busy work," as well as the amount of time that was needlessly waisted by others. Of course, if I was totally honest with the analysis of my audit, it also brought to light the amount of time that I spent needlessly bothering others.

Yes, regardless of the audit used, it will take time. The payoff of which will be determined by how serious one is to obtain the information that can have an impact of both our life and the productive value we can offer.

Accountability

It is a fact of life that we are all accountable to someone. Parents hold their children accountable, and parents are accountable for the well-being of their children. Both teachers and students, as well as employees and employers are accountable to each other.

However, because we have 100% control over how we spend our time, when it comes to time management our primary accountability is to ourselves. If we fail in our responsibility to accept the accountability we have for the management of our time, it will soon become evident that we have failed not only in the control we have over our time, but even more importantly, the control that we have in the destiny of where our career and our life will lead us.

No one can say with any degree of honesty or certainty, that they are in control of their life until they can say with a degree of certainty that they are in control of their time. The successful management of time is the first and foremost mindset that we must adopt if we hope to have the mindset of those who are successful, and for us to become our best rendition.

I would invite you to review once again the area of success that you stated as your primary objective. Now ask yourself:

- Am I managing my time in such a way that it is helping me or hindering me in accomplishing this objective?
- Am I managing my time in such a fashion that will permit me

to bring the most to the table?

- Am I managing my time so that it will enable me to become the best rendition of myself?
- Do I manage my time in such a manner that I remain the master of it, rather than it being the master of me?

How you answer these four questions will be the as true test as to the accountability you have accepted for the management of your time.

12

Creative Thinking

In this chapter, we'll discuss another indispensable mindset of successful people. It's one that should be considered crucial to the overall control one can have over their career, their life, and for sure their ultimate destiny.

This mindset is also a significant factor needed in the regeneration of our positive magnetic energy for the Power of our Positive Thinking that creates the Inspirational thoughts that come our way. As the title of this chapter indicates the mindset I am referring to consists of our ability to *"Think Creatively."*

As the theme for his campaign for the presidential nomination in 1968, Senator Robert F. Kennedy used a quote that was very similar to one made by George Bernard Shaw some 20 years earlier when he said, *"Some men see things as they are and say, why; I dream of things that never were and say, why not."* [20] This theme was such a part of his campaign, and how he thought as a person, that his brother Ted also used it as the theme when delivering Senator Kennedy's eulogy.

Creative thinking is the ability to bring more to the table by creatively looking at things the way they could be and saying, "Why not?" when others are simply saying "Why?" Or worse yet, they're not saying anything at all, but only accepting things as they are without accepting the responsibility to take control. Creative Thinking is the fruits that results from our Positive Thinking, of which as was said, becomes the breeding ground that provides the environment for the creative Inspiration we receive.

Creative thinking has two primary components:

- ✓ *Component #1* consists of our ability to creatively arrive at new opportunities to improve upon the way we are currently doing things, thus saying "Why not?" and as a result enabling us to bring more to the table.
- ✓ *Component #2* consists of our ability to creatively arrive at solutions to situations or issues that may be standing in our way, or at a minimum slowing us down from accomplishing our objective, thus again enabling us to bring more to the table.

To simplify the difference, consider component #1 as the creative inspiration that motivates us to act upon the "new and improved version" of an existing way of doing business; the better "mousetrap," if you will. Whereas component #2 is the creative inspiration that motivates us to focus and act upon resolving a problem or issue that is hampering us or standing in the way of doing business. Of course, both components can and should also be used in various facets of our

---

[20] http://politicaldog101.com/2018/03/robert-kennedy-did-george-bernand-shaw/

personal lives as well.

When creative thinking is not the focused mindset, there are typically three opposing mindsets that become dominant in one's life. They consist of; destructive thinking, worry, and the status quo.

Destructive Thinking

The first opposing mindset is that of negative thinking which often can evolve into destructive thinking. This mindset is without a doubt negative magnetic energy generating at its peak performance.

As an example, a teacher who should have a positive mindset of how to captivate the minds of the students, but instead has a mindset with a focus on how unmanageable the children are today, or how difficult it is to deal with the so-called helicopter parents, will eventually evolve into destructive thinking.

I recall a time when I belonged to a Business Referral Network Group. We met for a luncheon meeting twice a month. The group consisted of about 30 professionals from various businesses in the community. Our focus was twofold. First, as the title suggested, was to give and receives referrals, but the second, and maybe even as the most valuable, was to be a support by providing encouragement, motivation, and inspiration to each other. But then there was Bill (not his real name). We all know a Bill. Bill was nice guy, but he was also a real downer to be around. Bill's primary mindset was that of being consistently negative. Instead of having a creative focus on ways in which to increase business, he instead complained about how demanding his clients were. He focused on how bad or slow the economy was, or how a competitor was undercutting him. He could come up with a thousand other issues that he could rationalize as to why his business is not as it should be, and it was quite obvious it wasn't.

When a negative mindset becomes the norm, instead of creatively focusing on how to make things better, or how things could be, or to have our minds being receptive to our next great Inspiration, people like Bill focus on most every situation in a negative way. Their focus is to lay the blame on others, or society, or the industry, or the company, or the economy, or competitors, or whatever.

With a negative mindset, we tend to look for and try to find fault with everything and anything that may be offered as a possible solution to the issues or situations as we envision them to be.

The sad part is, after we have lived with this mindset for any extended period, we tend to become so good at it that we can now use it as an excuse or justification for not moving forward to become the best rendition of ourselves. We have become so comfortable with this mindset that we find no need or desire for generating the positive magnetic energy that will change our thought process. Needless to say, without positive magnetic energy being generated, any positive inspirations will also be blocked. If by chance it does make its way through, it will not be recognized or for sure acted upon.

Then to compound it even more, we often seek out others who have the same negative mentality. We soon find ourselves joining those "others" who congregate around the water cooler or at that corner table at lunch to discuss how bad things are. There is a lot of truth in the statement that "misery loves company."

For a person like Bill, who has a persistent negative outlook, it does not take long before their entire demeanor becomes negative and they soon evolve to the degree that their negative thinking turns into destructive thinking. As is often the case, whereas a person with negative thinking may prevent themselves from moving forward, a person with destructive thinking also has a desire to stop others from moving forward.

Worry

The second opposing mindset that can set in is that of worry. Not only what we worry about but also why we worry.

I consider myself a real worrywart. Truth be known, I am no ordinary worrywart. It's a trait I have not only inherited from my mother, but I have practiced it, improved it, and advanced it to the point that I think I have become a master at it.

For Centuries we have been told that worry is of no value, as it does not change a thing. Even in the Bible Jesus said, *"Do not worry about tomorrow for tomorrow will take care of itself."* He also said, *"Who of you, by your worry, can add but a single moment to your life span?*

George Bernard Shaw once said, *"People become attached to their burdens sometimes more than the burdens are attached to them."*

There is a Swedish Proverb that says, *"Worry often gives a small thing a big shadow."*

A study was cited in an article published by the National Institute of Mental Health,[21] in which they mention several adverse effects that worry and anxiety can have on our life. In summary, they reported that generalized worry & anxiety disorder symptoms include:
- Feeling of restlessness, wound up, or on edge
- Being easily fatigued
- Having difficulty concentrating; mind going blank
- Being Irritable
- Having sleep problems, such as difficulty falling or staying asleep, restlessness, or unsatisfying sleep

But we still do it..... So, the question then is Why? Why, after all the advice and studies that proves worry has no value, why are so

---

[21] www.nimh.nih.gov/health/topics/anxiety-disorders

many of us so good at it.

If someone says to me, "you really shouldn't worry about that," aren't they really saying that I should not think about it? But how can I do that? If something is weighing on my mind, how can I not help but think about it? If I tell myself that I should not think about it, am I also telling myself that it's not all that important to me. But then I circle around to the point that if I did not care about it, and if it was not that important to me, then why is it weighing on my mind?

So, how can we not think about an issue that is weighing on our minds? Maybe the answer is that we are only kidding ourselves when we try not to. But how do we do that and yet not worry?

If we dissect and carefully analyze most any issue we may be worried about, we will usually discover it's a problem or an issue that we do not have the degree of control we desire.

For me, I have found that the issues I worry about most fall into one of two general categories. Number one are those issues that are not within my ability to fix. The list of such examples is countless, but let's use as our example the subject of a loved one who is wrestling with either a debilitating or life-limiting illness. This is an example that is virtually impossible for us not to think about and have it weighing heavily on our mind. So, it causes us to worry even though we can do nothing about it. It is not fixable, anyway by us.

The second category consists of those fixable issues and challenges we can face on almost a daily basis. We have a challenging issue at work and not sure how it will resolve itself, so we worry about it. We are wrestling with a relationship issue and not sure what to do about it, so it causes us to worry.

Regardless if it is an issue that is fixable or not, because it has a degree of importance to us, it will naturally weigh on our mind to one degree or another. And for someone to suggest we should not worry about it does not help.

The issues we tend to worry about covers a wide range of anxieties, from the catastrophic, to that of what can be in the category of the more everyday concerns.

As it relates to the catastrophic worries of which we seldom have control, how to mentally address these issues requires a more indebt discussion than is intended to be given in a book such as this. So instead lets focus our discussion on the more everyday worry that most of us are susceptible to. This is the worry that we deal with regarding the matters we face in both our personal and professional life. These are the issues that will impact our journey toward becoming our best rendition.

Several chapters back, we discussed the fact that we, as humans, have the power to change what it is that we are thinking by merely deciding to do so. Changing what we are thinking about is not the same as not thinking about something. But still, it will be of little help to my psyche if I try to change my thoughts from a difficult issue I am facing to that of sipping a cocktail on a beach in the Caribbean.

But what I can do, is to change the focus of my thoughts from the problem or issue, to a focus on potential resolutions for those fixable problems.

Worry occurs when our mind is fixated on the problem. When that is our only reaction, we can be guaranteed that we are shutting down all possibility of producing the creative Inspiration that could resolve the situation. Worry is the anesthesia to our mind that block those positive, inspiring thoughts that may come our way. The funny thing is those inspirations that are blocked because of our worry could likely be the very answer to resolve the issue we are worrying about.

When worry becomes our norm, our mind tells our brain that we are helpless. Our mind tells our brain that we have no control over the situation, so we might just as well throw in the towel and take our ball and go home because there is little or no hope. Worry shuts down any and all Faith, Trust, and Confidence. Our mind tells our brain that our situation or issue exceeds our ability to resolve it. As a rule, fear of the unknown heightens our anxiety of which breeds even greater deep-seated worry.

The Status Quo

The third major roadblock that prevents the creative thinking that generates positive inspiration is when people become satisfied with the status quo of their career or life. For these people, instead of creatively thinking of greater possibilities as to how they can become their best of themselves, they instead are satisfied with the way things are. Well, although they may not be totally satisfied, but they're content enough with their current status quo that they have elected not to put forth the creative effort and energy that might implement a positive change.

While there is absolutely nothing wrong with being satisfied with our current state in life, in fact reaching this point in life is an integral part of our definition of success. However, there is a difference between having a feeling of fulfillment and satisfaction compared to simply settling at a level of contentment because we have convinced ourselves "That's the best it will ever get, so why even try?" Once we convince ourselves that we have reached our maximum potential of what life has to offer, it is then that it just becomes easier to accept the status quo.

Consider all the advancements we as a society would have missed out on if it were not for someone taking the initiative, and yes, sometimes even the risk to think creatively with a focus on greater possibilities. Although change just for the sake of change may not always be a good thing but change with a focus on growth and improvement *is* a good thing.

The reality is that the "status quo" is seldom a favorable option. Being satisfied with where you are at today or even an attitude of doing things the way you have always done them merely means that you have put your brain in neutral and made the decision to hit the delete button on any positive inspiration that may come your way. When this becomes the case, you can be almost guaranteeing that the rest of the world may have already passed you by. When this is the case you become certifiable as a Master Flee Trainer.

Regardless of where we are at in life, regardless of what we are doing or the objective we have as our focus, the reality is such that we only have one of four general mindsets from which our mind can instruct our brain to develop. To summarize:

Mindset #1 is to focus on the negative, which will always guarantee to push away any creative and positive Inspirational thoughts

Mindset #2 is to worry, which will cause us to adopt the mindset that we are helpless and have no control; therefore, the best we can do is merely hang on and accept things as they are. Worry is the anesthesia that numbs the brain, thus preventing it from receiving any positive Inspiration.

Mindset #3 is to be satisfied with the status quo and willing to see the rest of the world pass you by. Even though in many instances the lid of that flee jar has been removed, yet our mindset for the status quo entraps us in the jar forever.

Mindset #4 is to develop a determination that instead of either "letting things happen" or "waiting for things to happen" or "worrying that things will or will not happen," we instead engage our positive magnetic energy to the degree that not only will generate as many creative Inspirational thoughts as possible, but equally as important it will give us the Faith, Trust, and Confidence to act upon the Inspirations that will come our way. Only then will we have any chance to take control of our career, our life, and our destiny.

The Adjusted Mindset

As stated and reinforced numerous times, the more positive magnetic energy we generate with a focus on producing a higher degree of creative thinking, the more creative and productive Inspirational thoughts we will attract. And the more that we draw to us, the more we will be drawn to them.

Regardless of our objective or the task at hand, success in all aspects of life will only come about because of finding more effective and productive ways of using our talents and abilities, thus becoming our best rendition.

Napoleon Hill once said, *"More gold is mined through the creative thoughts of man than is ever taken from the earth."* [22]

Regardless of our endeavors or the situation we may find ourselves with, the success that we can obtain once we come to the realization of the power that can result from our creative thinking, the Inspirational thoughts that are produced, and the possibilities they can offer, it can be almost beyond our imagination.

None of the miracles of modern medicine would have ever come about if it were not for the creative thinking and Inspiration that someone acted upon.

All the world's greatest inventions were the result of the creative thinking that resulted in producing the Inspiration for the better "mousetrap."

Creative thinkers who act upon their Inspirations become the leaders. These are the folks who will shine because they think outside

---

[22] https://www.brainyquote.com/quotes/napoleon_hill_152865

of the circles and they try to connect that which others often feel cannot be connected.

Creative thinkers don't stick their head in the sand and pretend that issues or situations do not exist; instead, they face reality. They focus on generating positive magnetic energy to boost the creative thinking that opens them to the inspiration that will assist them in arriving at options, possibilities, and opportunities that may be available.

But positive Inspiration does not only land at the doorsteps of the Nobel Prize winners of the world, the renowned leaders, or the captains of industry. As a society we have been greatly blessed by the contributions folks such as this have made as a result of acting upon the Inspiration they received. Yet we must never discount the tremendous value of the gift that we, as everyday people, of every walk-in life, make to our families, our churches, our companies, and indeed our entire communities when we generate Positive Thinking that will open our minds to receiving the Inspirations that are gifted to us. Which when acted upon will bring the success we seek for us to become our best rendition.

Your success toward becoming the best of yourself will be achieved by your acting upon that next creative Inspirational thought that will come your way. Hang on for the journey will be great, it will be exciting and for sure very rewarding. The success you will realize as the result of your inspiration will be in direct correlation as to what you do between that period of receiving the inspiration and when you act upon it. When we fail to develop the strength of our Faith, Trust, and Confidence in recognizing and acting on our inspirations is when we permit them to float away like precious diamonds floating down the stream.

I cannot stress enough the significance that creative thinking will have not only on your career, but also your life in general, and for sure your destiny.

I am reminded of a story that I read somewhere a long time ago about Henry Ford. As I remember it, the story goes that Mr. Ford was attending a conference with one of his senior executives. At this conference, they were listening to a presentation given by an individual, who without question was an intellectual. This speaker was able to cite all sorts of statistical information with supporting data. He had a perfect command of the English language, and it was evident he was well schooled in his area of expertise.

When the conference was over the senior executive commented how impressed he was with this presenter's level of intelligence. He then asked Mr. Ford, *"How much would you pay to have a person with such intelligence on your staff?"* Mr. Ford replied, *"$35."* (Now *remember when this was and the value of the dollar for that time)*. To which the executive asked, *"By $35 do you mean a day or a week, or what?" "No,"* replied Mr. Ford, *"I mean a one-time payment of $35."* The executive then challenged Mr. Ford as to how he could justify that sum. Ford told the executive that while this information is good, valuable and even vital, he wanted to surround himself with people who had a creative mind to put this information to use. Ford said that he wanted to surround himself with a staff who could put their creative minds together to achieve possibilities of which that highly intelligent person may not begin to fathom. He told his executive, *"If all I wanted was information, I can spend $35 to buy a set of encyclopedias. That's how I can justify a onetime payment of that amount"*

I challenge you to think of any highly successful person who is not a creative thinker in all aspect of his or her life.

Take someone like Bill Gates, who for many years had been reported as being the wealthiest man in the world. Although he may have been the richest, do you think he is also the smartest man in the world? No, in fact, I would bet that over the years he has had many others working for him who had a higher IQ than his. Yet consider how many of all those smarter people did not progress beyond the cubical they worked in. What set Bill Gates apart from the rest of the world is his ability to not only think creatively, but even more important his ability to accept, believe, trust, and of most importance, act upon the positive Inspirations that came his way.

When it comes to creative thinking and the creative inspirational thoughts that are generated, there is an important and even critical issue that is essential to be remembered. So make sure you take special note of this.

The more positive magnetic energy we generate, the more inspiring options and opportunities will be presented to us. I remind you, often these creative thoughts are like diamonds floating down a stream. If we don't capture them as they come our way, they will usually disappear forever.

Once that breath of inspiration comes upon us, we need to immediately capture them by recording in whatever way is most useful for us. If we don't, as I said, like diamonds in a stream, chances are they will disappear forever.

How many times has it happened that you are involved in an important project at work or a personal project when suddenly, out of nowhere, a great inspiration comes into your mind about how you could improve or advance the project? It's an idea that you had never entertained before. It was like a flash, and when that inspirational thought entered your brain, you felt quite sure it could be a great idea that's at least worth further pursuit. But you failed to record the idea and later that day or the next, for the life of you, you cannot recall what it was. All you can remember is that at the time it felt like a great idea.

This same situation can also happen to us during the night, and sometimes even more so. You go to bed with a challenge weighing heavy on your mind. Then at some point during the night you were awakened by an inspirational thought that was so great that you almost found yourself sitting straight up in bed. But again, you failed to record it, and as is so often the case, by the next morning all you can remember is that you know it was an awe expiring idea, so much so that it made you excited at the time. It was a real inspiration, it was a true gift, but you failed to act upon that gift, so it floated away.

With the technology that's available to us today, making notes and memos to ourselves has become so simple that we are crazy not to do it. The smartphones of today offer so many different apps for us to either write, dictate or otherwise record every one of our creative Inspirational thoughts before we lose them.

Think about it: If our positive magnetic energy is attracting these inspiring creative inspirational thoughts and ideas to us, why in the world would we want to let them simply float away? Yet isn't that what we do so often?

13

Mastermind

When we have a focus on becoming our best rendition, there will be those times when we need more creative power than our personal positive magnetic energy can generate by itself. When this happens, we need to join the creative Inspiration we receive to that of the creative Inspiration received by others. When we are faced with a big job, it's only logical that we need to increase the horsepower to accomplish the objective at hand.

When two or more people engage their positive, creative thinking with a focus on the same objective that is when we increase the horsepower. That's when the sparks from their combined positive magnetic energy will begin to fly. It is then that creativity and new possibilities are substantially multiplied over that of when only a single person has the same focus.

Whenever this is done, this creates what is referred to as a

"Mastermind." Or we can also call it a *"think tank"* or a *"brain trust."* Regardless of what we call it, we typically refer to this activity as *"brainstorming."*

Try picturing in your mind what the weather is typically like when it is "storming." We know that storms can have incredible power. Storms can have a way of changing the landscape, and the greater the storm, the more significant change it can produce. Even when we experience a lesser storm, such as an everyday thunderstorm, it doesn't take long before we know there will be some impact to the locale of the storm.

The same thing happens when a mastermind engages the power of a brainstorming session. Seldom do we stop to recognize and appreciate its power, much less use its power to our advantage to improve things.

Several times throughout this book I have invited you to visualize the power of the magnet. Again, I would ask that you consider what happens when several magnets are used and the additional power the combined magnets can have over that of just one.

In the same way that multiple magnets will have more power to attract over that of a single magnet, so too when numerous people combine their positive magnetic energy to form a mastermind, this combined effort of the mastermind can produce an unbelievably power toward raising the bar to arrive at new and creative ways to look at things, new ways to accomplish objectives, and new ways to resolve issues.

Consider this simple scenario as an example. It's common for most television sitcoms to have a cadre of four to six writers who lock themselves in a room so they can creatively come up with the script for the next show. They begin by creating the basic plot. Then they work out the involvement of the various characters and the role each will have in the overall show. From that big picture they then begin a focus on the details of writing the lines of the script for the involvement of each character.

This cadre of writers are continually bouncing things off each other. Because one idea may spur another, in most instances, how the plot is ultimately played out will look and feel altogether different from the initial vision, and in most cases viewed as being better. It is totally due to the brainstorming power of this mastermind of the combined creativity of the writers that resulted in the creation of the final production.

It is this same creative brainstorming that is accomplished when a mastermind tackles many of the everyday issues of business.

Going back to consider the creative mastermind of the sitcom writers. Since most sitcoms today are recorded and aired later, the writers are typically not under the same degree of pressure as they were in the days when most shows were broadcast as a live performance every week. With live programming, occasionally the writers could find themselves in a situation whereby they had to revise their finished scripts by quickly rewriting a new scene. For example, if one of the performers fell unexpectedly ill, the mastermind was faced with a real crisis that needed to be resolved. Not resolving the issue was not an option. The brainstorming needed to be kicked into high gear to rewrite the script, for as the saying goes, "The show must go on."

The mastermind is most powerful when it is used to resolve an issues or situations that may be preventing either an individual entity or even an entire group from advancing as they need to, want to, or hope to.

Whenever a mastermind engages in brainstorming to resolve an issue or situation, it must begin with the firm conviction of the reality that there *is no such thing as an issue o*˞ *problem that does not have a resolution.* Without a doubt, every successful person has this well ingrained as part of the foundation of t˥eir mindset: *There is a resolution to every issue or problem.*

That's a critical reality that we must alwεys understand. *There is a resolution to every issue or problem. There is a resolution to every issue or problem.* Tell your mind to ingrain that permanently into your brain. There is *a resolution to every issue or problem.* There is no situation, issue, or problem where there is nɔt a resolution. None... Never... There is always a resolution to every issue or problem.

Consider for a minute the number of illnesses throughout history that were at one time considered to be incurable... *There is a resolution to every issue or problem.*

The day will come, and that day could in all likelihood happen in our lifetime when there will be a cure for every cancer. *There is a resolution for every issue or problem.*

Consider that whenever a natural disaster strikes, regardless of the degree of tragic loss and heartbreak that was experienced, given time, the damages are repaired, and ife continues. *There is a resolution to every issue or problem.*

Consider all the major wars and political conflicts throughout history. *There is a resolution to every issue or problem.*

There has never been an issue, situatior, or problem at any time throughout history that, in time, was not resolved in one way or another. *There is a resolution to every issue, situation or problem, and for every issue, situation, or problem that has ever existed throughout history, there was always someone or a group of those someone's who had arrived at how it could be resolved.*

Consider how many times throughout the week we encounter issues or situations in either our professional or personal lives in which we initially conclude that there is no resolution, and because of that mindset, we delay or never develop a determination to seek a resolution.

The well-known author Napoleon Hill first introduced the Mastermind concept in his book *The Law of Success*[23] that was first published in 1928. Throughout his career, he advocated the use of mastermind groups as a way of taking your personal and professional life to the next level. In his book, he originally promoted that, *"When two or more people get together to focus on an issue, a third mind, the Master Mind was created."* To emphasize the usefulness of a mastermind group, he compared it to one who connects a bank of electric batteries to a single transmission wire thereby substantially increasing the energy needed. Hill observed that *"Each mind, through the principle of mind chemistry, stimulates all the other minds in the group."* In our discussion here we have been referring to that very thing as another example of "magnetic energy."

Business and career coach Susan Ascher commented on the value and importance of a mastermind group by saying. *"Mastermind groups have improved the way people do business. They enable individuals with lofty goals to take real, actionable steps toward achieving them. Brainstorming with like-minded people in a group setting is beneficial for all involved. There's a reason mastermind groups are still alive today... they actually work. The list of potential benefits one can get from a mastermind group is virtually endless."*[23]

When done correctly by the right people with the right mindset, one should never underestimate the creative power the mastermind can have in generating new positive, creative ideas for building a better mousetrap, or to resolve issues or develop solutions that may

---

[23] *The Law of Success* by Napoleon Hill, published by The Penguin Group 1928. Originally published as an eight-volume set.

be hampering business growth and progress. There is a thought that is often attributed to St. Francis of Assisi that says; *"First do what is necessary, then do what is possible, and before long you will be doing what is impossible."* When done right, this is what a mastermind is all about. It is accomplishing what is often thought of as the *"impossible."*

Although the establishing of a formal mastermind can produce enormous benefits, yet in smaller organizations such a formal setting may be somewhat impractical. That does not mean that a smaller group cannot benefit from the power or a master mind. In fact, it is done every day.

Think of when two or three doctors who put their minds together every day so they can best arrive not only at a proper diagnosis but also an effective treatment plan.

Think of the engineers who by putting their heads together arrive at a workable design that one engineer alone may not have come up with in a thousand years.

A bit earlier I mentioned that I had been a member of a Business Referral Network Group. I also mentioned that our focus was twofold. First, it was to give and receives referrals amongst each other. But the second was to be a support by providing encouragement, motivation, and inspiration to each other. I also mentioned that although generating referrals was important, yet what had often proved to be of the most value is when the group acted as a Master Mind.

As members of the group we were encouraged to bring business issues that to one degree or another we were struggling with. At first the issues were simple everyday problems. However, the longer that we as a group were together, the more trusting relationships we developed. This resulted in an increase in the comfort level we had in sharing more problematic issues.

It was not unusual for us as a group to spend two, three or more of our luncheon sessions with a focus the same issue presented by one of our members. As a group we had a firm understanding that "there is a resolution to every issue or problem" therefore we would spend as many sessions and time necessary to arrive at ideas and suggestions for potential resolution.

Needless to say, our group did not have the same degree of "skin in the game" as would a Mastermind Group consisting of employees within a company, or even if all the members were of the same industry. Having said that however, in most every instance, regardless of how big or small the issue, the results of our Mastermind Group was successful at generating the spark of Inspiration necessary for thoughts and ideas to either form a likeminded Mastermind Group or the final resolution.

Here is the bottom line: It makes no difference if you are generating your own personal positive magnetic energy, or if it's the combined creative power of a formal mastermind group, or the collaborative thoughts of two or more individuals. The difference between using it or not is often the difference between taking control of the situation or just letting the situation control you. It's usually about doing what many would consider as the impossible. It's the difference between becoming the best version of yourself or merely settling for mediocrity. The absolute key, however, is that the issue must be approached with the firm conviction that *there is a resolution to every issue or situation.*

There are always options for not accepting the status quo, and those options will only present themselves when we do what is necessary to take control by generating our positive magnetic energy.

Regenerating for Maximum Power

Thus far we have discussed various mindsets that successful people have formed and maintain as the paradigm of their lives. Understanding their mindsets and the paradigm that they create are necessary if we wish to have any degree of control over all aspects of our life.

I'm sure you have already concluded that it takes consistent and strong positive magnetic energy to maintain a positive paradigm. But as with any energy, if it is not recharged or regenerated, it will lose its power.

If, for example, I turn the headlights of my car on but do not run the engine to recharge the battery, sooner or later the lights will go out because I had drained the energy from the battery

Therefore, the more Inspiration and opportunities we desire for our positive magnetic energy to attract to us, the stronger that magnetic force must be. That magnetic force can only become stronger when we do what is necessary to generate more of it, and that takes recharging.

If you recall earlier when we defined success, we said that life is such that *"we can only have and receive more when we become more."* We also said that the more fulfillment and satisfaction that we experience in what we do, the deeper the passion we will have for what we are doing. The point was made that this in turn will produce a stronger desire to become more, which will motivate for us to do more, and the more we do, the more we will receive.

This all relates directly to the amount of positive magnetic energy that we generate. This regeneration is accomplished through several different avenues.

Balance

A critical component in becoming our best rendition is the need to have a balance in all aspects of our life. The greater the balance, the more likely we will achieve the destiny we desire. But balance seldom happens by accident. It's a fact that the realities of life today can be complicated, if not difficult at times. To counter the complexities of the issues of life, control is necessary, and maintaining a balance in all aspects of our lives is an essential product of our control.

At best, it is difficult for anyone to have a focus on recharging or regenerating positive magnetic energy and to accept positive inspiration when life is out of balance. When life feels that it is balanced that is usually an indication that things are running relatively smooth. Generally speaking, whatever area is out of balance and not running smoothly, it is likely that it will cause other areas of life to sooner or later be also affected.

Consequently, keeping all aspects of our life in balance is a primary key to maintaining control. Balance is key to our ability to regenerate our positive magnetic energy.

Balance = Control = Positive Magnetic Energy

Education

Another important way to regenerate our positive magnetic energy is by seeking greater knowledge through more education in the area of our endeavors. But all too often we are so busy and so focused on the issues of today that we fail to look for the very tools that could take us to the next level.

A physician friend once told me, "Dan, in just a few hours I can teach you how to perform an appendectomy. However," he said, "It will take me four years to train you what to do if something goes wrong."

He naturally was referring to both the necessity and the value of medical school, passing of all the test, and receiving the medical degree. But his same point could apply to virtually every profession or job, and indeed, even life in general. In the world we live in today, our education cannot end once we get that diploma, degree, certification, or license. To keep on top of our game and become our best rendition continued education is an absolute must.

It is quite common that for most any profession that requires a license, certification, or other credentialing, continuing education is a requirement to maintain those credentials. Unfortunately, when it comes to going after that continued education our motivation to do so is often lacking. eH

We get so busy and so tied down in the everyday battle of what we are doing that we fail to stop long enough to replenish the nutrients that feed not only our creativity but also the motivation to take on the day. The popular, well-known business consultant and author John Maxwell observed that *"The unsuccessful person is burdened by learning and prefers to walk down familiar paths. Their distaste for learning stunts their growth and limits their influence."*[2]

Continued education does not have to be a burden; it does not have to be boring; it does not have to be something that we "have to do." Like anything else in life, it's a matter of purpose and attitude. Regardless if it is an advanced degree or a four-hour workshop, it's a matter of attitude and looking for the priceless pearl, as there will usually be one.

I challenge you to think of any endeavor that you have ever had the desire to accomplish. Maybe it involved your career, a personal project, or even a hobby or pastime. Whatever it was, I am sure that you have noticed that the more passion you have for it, the easier it was to learn more about it. The fact is, the higher the passion we have toward whatever our interest or endeavor may be, the easier it will be to regenerate our positive magnetic energy by seeking further education. Knowledge becomes the catalyst for the inspiration that comes our way. So again, just like that of a magnet, this in turn both draws us into the education as well as drawing that knowledge gained to us.

Not only does it come more naturally, but because of the enhanced inspiration and motivation we will gain, we will experience an increased enjoyment of the journey of going after it. This will lead into becoming even more fired up about the endeavor, all of which leads to an even deeper passion.

I have a good friend who suffered from a severe illness during his early childhood. As a result, he missed a considerable amount of school during his first and second grades. Due to the high fever that he often experienced, it resulted in making it more difficult for him to concentrate and learn at the same rate as the other children in his grade. Given that the education system was different some 60 years ago compared to today, my friend fell behind the rest of his class and remained so throughout his entire elementary and high school years. As a result, he absolutely hated school, which also resulted in his learning difficulty being compounded. To this day he will tell you that he has never finished reading a book in its entirety.

The funny thing is, he has an absolute passion for motorcycles. This has been a passion of his for more than two decades. As a result, He subscribes to almost every motorcycle magazine on the market. He not only reads every issue, but he studies them to the degree that he is probably the most well-versed individual on every motorcycle on the market today. He not only is knowledgeable of every make and model, but he can recite almost all the specs of each.

However, motorcycles were not his only passion in life. He also had a passion for his chosen profession and had the same degree of intensity toward learning all he could in that area.

Although he may have found "book" learning to be very difficult, yet due to his street smarts, his degree of common sense, and his ability to think things through, combined with his desire to learn all he could in the area of his specific passionate interest, he went on to be very successful in his chosen career.

Isn't that precisely what we're talking about when speaking of generating positive magnetic energy?

In almost every instance, whenever we find ourselves in a stalemate position with something that we may have once had a burning passion for, one of the most effective ways to reignite that flame is to begin once again focusing on learning more about it.

For example, say you're finding your career is in a bit of a stalemate. If you are serious and have a sincere desire to reignite that flame, then try delving into updating your skills by seeking more education. Discover new technology that may help you do your job better or become more efficient.

Try refocusing and learning new and positive avenues of where your career can take you and how you can enhance the value of your job.

Through further education try focusing on how you can creatively bring more to the table and become more valuable to your employer, your fellow employees, and all the stakeholders your position brings you in contact with.

The more education you pursue in each of these areas, the more positive magnetic energy it will generate. Education opens our minds so that we can recognize the value of the inspirations that come our way.

The same holds true regardless of the endeavor. If finance is an area that you sincerely have a desire to improve, then try reading some of the many books, or attending classes and seminars offered by financial experts that provide both insight and motivation.

If improving relationships or resolving family issues is your greatest desire or need at this juncture of your life, then read and learn of the potential options and suggestions available from some of the many experts in that field.

The more education we seek, regardless of the endeavor, the more positive magnetic energy we will generate, and the more we will both recognize and value our inspired creativity. All of which becomes an ever-increasing and widening spiral of success.

The Proactive Mentality

Another prime example of how we can regenerate more positive magnetic energy and open ourselves to greater inspiration lies in our ability to be proactive in all aspects of our life.

Each of us has the power to develop this ability. We have the power to put into action whatever is necessary to achieve the goals and objectives that will ultimately produce our best rendition.

Being proactive is when you do what you can to make things happen instead of adapting to a situation or just waiting for things to happen.

In the mid '80s I transitioned from a Real Estate Broker to a Contractor/Developer. I made that transition by first joining the staff of a reputable general contractor in our area who had the desire to transition from a General Contractor to more of a Design/Build Developer. Now during the early to mid-80's our Country was still in the midst of an economic stand still. Not much was happening in terms of growth. But by the two of us joining forces, we became determined that we were not going to let that stand in our way. We were determined that we would take control of our destiny and do whatever we could to make things happen rather than waiting for things to happen.

Without a doubt it took a lot of hard work and long hours, not to mention a lot of Faith, Trust and Confidence in the Inspirations that landed at our doorsteps, but together we turned that little company into one with sales that exceeded 80,000,000.

When we do what we can to make things happen, we take control by acting versus merely reacting.

Being proactive is the difference between managing our life by objective versus managing life from one crisis to another. It's the difference between accepting the responsibility to do what we can versus doing nothing and then play the "poor me" victim.

In business, being proactive means that we place a greater emphasis on forward-thinking by making calculated plans to meet market changes, customer and client expectation, the ever evolving and changing economy, or a host of other issues that exist.

An excellent example of this is with the Converse Shoe Company, a manufacture that had been around for virtually 100 years. But they were stuck and did very little forward thinking. During the third quarter of 2001, they reported losses of $5.4 million. They even resorted to selling their corporate headquarter building to reduce debt.

But then came Nike, a competitor who bought Converse in 2003. Nike immediately embarked on a campaign of forward-thinking. They did a complete rebranding of this 100-year-old company. They collaborated with artists and designers to come up with a staggering number of shoe varieties that would appeal to the consumer of today.

When Nike first purchased the company in 2003, Converse's annual sales landed at just over $200 million. Due to Nike's forward thinking, by 2016 annual sales for Converse reached almost $2 billion. That's the power of positive forward thinking. That's the power of making things happen instead of just waiting for things to happen.

Your Magnetic Energy

In our personal life, being proactive means that we take whatever steps we can to not only meet our needs of today but that we also plan for both our future and the future of our family. Being proactive means having a focus on growth, regardless if it's in our relationships, our finances, our personal and spiritual growth, or whatever, versus simply accepting thing as they are and settling for the status quo.

Whether in business or our personal life, being proactive is the difference between taking charge and doing what we can to make positive things happen that is in our best interest, or just settling for whatever comes our way.

Being proactive and doing what is necessary to make positive things happen is when our positive magnetic energy is working at its peak performance to generate the inspirational thoughts and ideas we need to become the best rendition of ourselves.

Because there is no limit as to the amount of positive magnetic energy that we can generate, it also logically follows that there is no limit to the proactive opportunities that will land at our doorsteps through the Positive Inspiration sent to us.

14

Conclusion

Redefine the Image We Have of Ourselves

Earlier it was discussed that our beliefs and the convictions that we hold to be true about ourselves would ultimately dictate our destiny. We acknowledged that our brains would think whatever our minds tell it to think, and when our minds repeat to our brains the same thoughts over some time, that thought process then becomes the paradigm of the mindset for which we live our life.

Now that sounds so simple, and it would be simple if that is all we had to do. But there is more to it than that. The problem isn't with the inability of our minds telling our brains what to think; the question comes when our minds may not be genuinely convinced or believe that which we are trying to say to our brains. We need to understand that our brains are not stupid. Our brains will never believe what our mind is telling it unless our mind believes it first.

Your Magnetic Energy

American Sociologist Charles Cooley points out that as a general rule, we tend to operate with the thought process of, "I am not what *I think* I am. I am not what *you think* I am. Rather I am what *I think you think I am*."

When that is the case, of which it is so often, aren't we turning much of the control of our career, our life and our destiny over to others? The key as to the degree of our ultimate control is for us to be the person, not of who we may think others think we are, but rather the person who we know, and have a firm conviction of who we are. Whenever we try to be the person who we think others think we are, we find ourselves trying to hit a moving target. There is no control in that.

In many instances, the reason we so often fail to have our mind send to our brain the right message is for the same reason that we often tend to listen too much to what we think others are thinking of us. Typically, these situations come into play when we lack clarity of who we are and where we wish to go. Without that clarity, without that focus, we have little or no control.

To grab ahold of that brass ring of life and to maintain control of our destiny, it's crucial that we have a clear understanding and a solid belief of who we are and the direction we are heading.

By far the best way to have that clarity of understanding and that focus is for us to have a one-on-one, heart to heart discussion with ourselves. No text, no emails, no message left in voice mail, just a simple old fashion one-on-one, heart to heart discussion. This is a discussion that clearly defines the image we have of ourselves. After all, it is that image that our mind is trying to convince our brain of what to believe. If we are happy and believe the image we have of ourselves, then we are on our way. If not, then we need to do what is necessary to generate all the positive magnet energy that we can muster to change it. Is that always easy? No, it's not always easy, *but it is still possible.*

I was born and raised on a small family farm. I moved off the farm some 50 years ago. Let me assure you, back then there were no creature comforts on the typical family farm, especially one the size of ours. The only labor-saving device that my dad had to do the outside chores was the three of us boys.

Whenever we would complain about something being too hard, or it being too cold, or too hot, or too heavy, or whatever we could come up with to complain about, we could expect the same answer. Dad would say; "if it were that easy, I'd get one of the lightweights to do it, but none of them showed up today." Then he would customarily follow by saying, "Now quit lollygagging and complaining and get back to work."

So, I conclude by saying to you. Is it easy? No, life itself is not always easy. If it were that easy the lightweights would be called in to do it, but usually they don't show up.

But you did show up, and you did so because you are not a lightweight. If you were a lightweight, you would not have spent your time and energy reading this book. Now it's up to you to do it. It will only be a waste of your time if you are waiting for the lightweights, or anyone else to step in and do it for you. The ball is totally in your court.

Chuck Swindoll, the Evangelical Christian pastor who founded *Insight for Living* which aired a radio program of the same name on more than 2,000 stations around the world once said, *"Light won't automatically shine upon you nor will truth silently seep into your head by means of rocking-chair osmosis. It's up to you. It's your move."*

So, let's start generating whatever Positive Magnetic Energy that's necessary to produce the Inspiration, thoughts, and the motivation we need to regain if necessary, and then to maintain the control that is essential to become the best rendition of ourselves that we were meant to be.

To echo the great quote from Zig Ziglar when he reminds us that *"we were designed for accomplishment, engineered for success, and endowed with the seeds of greatness."*

I would like to leave you with a final thought. Benjamin Disraeli who served two terms as the British Prime Minister in the mid to late 1800's once said, *"The greatest good you can do for another is not just to share your riches but to reveal to him his own."* The focus of this book is to provide various avenues for the journey toward becoming our best rendition. By building a solid foundation of Faith, Trust, and Confidence that will enable us to act upon the positive Inspirations we receive as a result of our Positive Magnetic Energy, we will truly come to recognize the true value and purpose of the talents and abilities we have been entrusted with. Never shy away from using the riches of what you can offer to the world. You were put on this earth for a reason. You have a specific purpose and more importantly, you have what it takes to fulfill both that reason and purpose.

As you contemplate the message of this book, I have no doubt you can think of members of your family, friends, co-workers, employees and associates who may also benefit from its message. Recommending it to others may be the spark for them to recognize the rough diamond they possess.

In echoing the quote from my dad, *"Now it's time to quit lollygagging and get to work"* on becoming your best rendition of who you were created to be and have the capability to become.

About the Author

Dan Hoeger believes that the most effective messenger is one who has lived the message. As such he brings to this book his 40 plus years of lived experience as a salesperson, a business entrepreneur and an employer. During which time, side by side with his professional career and active family life he was also an active leader in his church and both his local and regional community,

His career began at the tender age of 18 when he started as a Kirby Vacuum Cleaner Salesman. Within a few years, he was the owner of the Factory Direct Franchise and grew the business to having offices in four different cities.

In 1972 he sold the business and entered the Real Estate Profession. For the next 35 years his career had a focus on this arena as he evolved from that of a Salesperson to a Broker-Owner, and finally by the mid 80's to that of a Design/Build- General Contractor/Developer. At the time of his retirement, he was the CEO of a regional development company with sales that exceeded $80,000,000.

In addition to his busy and sometimes hectic professional career, plus a very active family, he was also very involved in both his church and community. In 1989 he was ordained as a Deacon of the Church. In 1991 the State's second largest newspaper ran a ½ page feature article on him that they entitled "A Capitalist and a Chaplain." The following year he was given the distinct honor of receiving a Governor's Volunteer of the Year Award.

As a result of being recognized as a reputable community leader, Dan was appointed or invited to become a member of numerous civic and faith-based committees, commissions and boards.

Dan has given talks and presentations consisting of keynote addresses, seminars, and workshops to corporations, churches, service organizations, schools, and other institutions

Dan and his wife Rosie have been married for over 50 years and make their home in Cedar Rapids, Iowa. They have six adult children whom they are very proud of. Each is married and successful in their respective careers. Their children have also blessed them with 13 beautiful grandchildren.

If you wish to reach Dan to discuss potential dates for a keynote address or other speaking engagement, or if you would like to pass on your thoughts and feedback regarding this book you are welcomed to contact him by email at Dan@DanHoeger.com

www.ingramcontent.com/pod-product-compliance
Lightning Source LLC
Chambersburg PA
CBHW020251030426
42336CB00010B/718